I SHOULD HAVE STAYED HOME
FOOD

Other Trouble Travel Collections from RDR Books

I Should Have Stayed Home: HOTELS
Hospitality Disasters at Home and Abroad

I Should Have Gone Home
Tripping Up Around the World

I Should Have Just Stayed Home
Award-winning Tales of Travel Fiascos

I Really Should Have Stayed Home
Worst Journeys from Harare to Eternity

I've Been Gone Far Too Long
Field Trip Fiascoes and Expedition Disasters

I Should Have Stayed Home
The Worst Trips of Great Writers

I SHOULD HAVE STAYED HOME
FOOD

Edited by Roger Rapoport,
Bob Drews & Kim Klescewski

RDR BOOKS
MUSKEGON, MICHIGAN

I Should Have Stayed Home: FOOD

RDR Books
1487 Glen Avenue
Muskegon, MI 49441
phone: 510-595-0595
fax: 510-228-0300
www.rdrbooks.com
email: roger@rdrbooks.com

Copyright 2007 by RDR Books
All Rights Reserved

ISBN: 978-1-57143-121-9

Library of Congress Control Number: 2006901667

Design and Production: Richard Harris
Cover Photograph: Dan Hare

Distributed in the United Kingdom and Europe by
Roundhouse Publishing Ltd., Millstone, Limers Lane,
Northam, North Devon EX39 2RG, United Kingdom

Distributed in Canada by
Scholarly Book Services, 127 Portland Street, 3rd Floor,
Toronto, Ontario, Canada M5V 2N4

Printed in the United States of America

CONTENTS

INTRODUCTION

When America's airlines suddenly decided to give up on serving food, trend spotters wondered what impact this might have on passengers' life expectancy. In one fell swoop, the carriers came up with the ultimate in low-salt, low-cholesterol fare, a menu guaranteed to help passengers lose weight. Sad to say, those of us who travel must, even if we are hung up on the tarmac for hours in bad weather, ultimately disembark and find something to eat.

As these pages suggest, we are forced to make tough decisions and adapt to foreign face-saving customs like the infamous Mao Tai rounds described in Alec LeSueur's piece. One of our faithful correspondents explains how a single misplaced pine nut can quickly turn the trip of a lifetime into a free ride to the emergency room. And in case you were wondering, the price you pay for a meal never guarantees a satisfactory dining experience. From waiters such as Sam Wo's legendary mean guy, Edsel Ford Wong, who never met

1

a customer he couldn't belittle, to the endangered species barbecue in the Amazon, this collection is sure to change your eating habits on the road.

If you're about to leave on a journey, this book will show you exactly how to avoid getting beaten up by your chef and manage to stay away from scary dishes that just might have you longing for a peanut butter and jelly sandwich. Keep an eye out for warning signs, such as a waiter unwilling to serve a nice au jus with your anteater. If you're in Italy, the home of slow dining, don't be surprised if you have to wait hours for the check. And please try not to eat the silkworms with your hands.

Down the Hatch

Clifford Pierce

How could we ever forget Tommy O'Leary, the Pan American Airways flight attendant who could sell a deep freeze to an Eskimo. A veteran from the days of the China Clipper, this short, cocky, wiry Irishman with the crinkly eyes could make a Tasmanian Devil smile. He could read his passengers, and he instinctively knew how to comfort the timid, placate the unhappy, cheer up the lonely and even get the white-knuckle crowd to soundly sleep their way through turbulence.

In the 1950s, on a B-377 Stratocruiser night flight from Manila to Guam one memorable passenger put him to the test. She was a lady, a matriarch, a person of enormous wealth accustomed to getting what she wanted. She could be very charming but you didn't want to be in the same room with her if she was really upset.

In Manila, Tommy was greeting passengers at the top of the boarding stairs, when she pulled herself up to him in a total snit. He had not been forewarned. Somewhere along the line a piece of her luggage had been misrouted, an irresponsible customs official had treated her as if she were an ordinary passenger and the flight was running about three hours late. At this point everyone she met in uniform was her enemy.

Before Tommy could smile and start to say, "Wel . . ." she spat out, "Now don't you welcome me, young man! I don't need any more of your damned 'Welcomes.' Just show me my seat, and tell the pilot that I should have left here three hours ago."

Eventually the Stratocruiser climbed out of Manila and flew east towards Guam in darkening skies. Still darker than the skies ahead was the lady's face. Tommy studied her and realized it was going to take some time to calm her down. But he knew he had the charm to turn her into a lifelong devotee of Pan Am. After all he was a legend in the company.

As soon as he could, Tommy sat beside her as she helped herself to a glass of sparkling wine and a platter of elegant hors d'oeuvres. He apologized for her previous difficulties and complimented her on her lovely muumuu and her youthful appearance. "Madam has flown on the Clipper Flying Boats? What wonderful childhood memories!" he said.

By the time she had finished her dinner, she was totally in his spell. Oh, that Tommy, he loved soothing difficult passengers.

The steward invited her to join him in the downstairs lounge where there was relaxing music on a 45 rpm record player and a special after-dinner drink. It was so special only he knew the recipe. She quickly descended the circular staircase into the U-shaped lounge down in the belly of the big Boeing and settled into the nest of pillows thoughtfully arranged by Tommy. At this moment there was not a happier, mellower passenger in the entire aircraft. The lounge was a private retreat where she alone would be treated like royalty.

In the small bar Tommy kept up the soothing chatter as

he carefully built, layer upon layer, his ultimate concoction, a masterpiece of four liqueurs carefully poured to make sure each layer did not mix with the others. It looked like a rainbow handcrafted by God.

She relaxed amidst among the pillows at the end of the lounge, as Tommy mixed his house specialty. Finally the Pan Am steward carried the inviting glass toward her on a silver tray, smiled, handed her the drink and mumbled something in French. She smiled back and raised the glass to her lips.

The Boeing Stratocruiser was originally designed as the B-29 Superfortress, the World War Two bomber that incinerated Hiroshima and Nagasaki. What better way to turn a sword into a plowshare than to make this military aircraft the perfect luxury transport. Alas, the Boeing engineers, in a rush to build the first postwar pressurized airline didn't have time to change every little hinge, snap and door latch.

Above the sole lounge passenger was an overhead ceiling panel that allowed the flight engineer to inspect hydraulic lines and wiring. The panel was about three feet long and a foot wide. It had a hinge at the back and was held in place by a sliding, spring-loaded latch.

Immediately after the distinguished passenger took her first sip of his exotic creation, the plane plowed through the top of a large cumulous cloud. Next he heard a "click" as the latch to the inspection panel slipped. Down swung the panel. Tommy made a desperate grab for it and missed. He watched as the panel swung in an arc, smacking the bottom of the glass in the demanding lady's hand.

The stemmed goblet and all four layers of its stratified contents, red, green, orange and brown, popped out of the lady's grasp, flipped over and disappeared down the front of her muumuu—glass and all.

In an emergency Tommy never had to be told what to do. He leaped forward and reached deep into her bodice to retrieve the glass. When he got his hand in far enough to grab it, the lady led out a shriek that could be heard clear up on the flight deck.

He quickly grabbed a bar towel, used it to wipe the mixed drink off her face, somewhat muffling the screams and then he stuffed it down her front. That's when she really screamed. He admitted later that he'd probably made a mistake following up so quickly after snatching the goblet out of her dress. Tommy fled up the stairs, brushing past two female flight attendants on their way down to check on this emergency.

During the next couple of weeks the mid-Pacific crisis became the subject of an internal inquiry reaching all the way to the top of the Chrysler Building, Pan Am's corporate headquarters in New York City. Tommy never got any medals, awards or thanks for slipping his hand down the lady's muumuu to retrieve the cocktail glass and then wiping up the mess. From his perspective he had "rescued" a valuable first class customer. Officially, the Pan Am Board of Directors apologized to the wronged lady. Privately, the details of Tommy's search-and-rescue operation became the subject of hilarious cocktail party chatter. When people asked Tommy about it, he refused to take credit for his simple act of inflight heroism.

"I was just doing my job."

KOREA'S SILK ROUTE

BY FRANK LEV

YOU DON'T SEE MANY OVERWEIGHT PEOPLE IN KOREA. That's because much of their diet is made up of greens and seaweed and other healthy fare. It seems like the best diet in the world, except for the shortage of fruit. There's only one problem for a foreigner. It's often hard to figure out whether the dish in front of you is animal, vegetable or mineral? And despite all the books I've read on Korean food, it is also a little tricky to figure out if the food is hot.

But if you're an adventurous eater, like me, dining out in Korea can be full of delightful surprises. I was walking around Namdaemon Shijang, the most famous market in Seoul, asking a friend to tell me what the vendors were offering. Each time she patiently explained the details, taking special delight in my reaction to exotic choices. I knew she was just waiting for me to break down and ask where I could find a good cheeseburger.

That was when I decided to try everything in Korea, even

if it looked, smelled or tasted weird. I vowed to try everything twice to graciously prove that I actually liked their food.

Of course, not everything in the Korean diet is a challenge. I found some great foods that I liked. One is called *hota*. It's a fat pancake with nuts and syrup inside cooked fresh on a very hot grill. You have to be careful because the syrup is so hot it can burn your skin. Fortunately, it doesn't burn the inside of your mouth. Please don't ask me to explain this. Then there was the candy that came in huge slabs shaved off with a machine that looked like a wood planer. It was delicious. Also there is the *ddok*, made from smashed rice that is turned into a playdough-type mixture. Inside they put a variety of fillings such as sweet black beans or sesame paste. Yum. Sometimes they just stew the ddok in a red sauce. Red, of course, is synonymous with hot sauce in Korea.

Koreans love to do strange things with squid and octopus, like creating a snack that looks like it was just run over by a steam roller. It is shiny (my friend said this is accomplished with a spray) and thin like a giant potato chip.

In the street stalls you can try many unusual items. There is obscene-looking ginseng. Mushrooms appear to be made out of plastic. And the peppers. The peppers are everywhere. It's what makes Korean food so distinctive and, well, hot. We went into a restaurant that specialized in *naengmyon,* or cold noodle soup. As you may know, when you go to a Korean restaurant they bring you side dishes you never ordered. Of course, *kim chi*, pickled cabbage, is present at every meal. The others items are usually mixed vegetables. To my surprise, after the soup was brought out, a waitress arrived with a pair of scissors and started cutting up our noodles to make them easier to eat.

Suddenly, another mystery dish that looked like a big bowl of brown nuts, aroused my curiosity.

"Oh, that," said my friend. "That's *bondegi*. It was my favorite when I was young." She gave me that funny half smile.

"I want to try one . . . one bondegi, *chuseyo*" (give me one please). I gingerly picked one up with my fingers. It looked like a small animal.

"Try it," she challenged. Defiantly I popped it in my mouth. It was crunchy and had a kind of smoky, nutty taste.

"What exactly is it?" I asked. My friend consulted with the stall owner and turned to her electronic dictionary.

"Ralva," she finally announced in triumph. "It's a ralva." I stopped and thought about what she said. Ralva. Ralva.

"Oh larva. You mean larva."

"Yes, yes. From a worm, a silkworm. It's a silkworm larva."

After downing one, I mustered all my willpower attained through many years of practicing yoga and meditation and said with conviction. "Hmm, not bad. May I have another?"

The two of us continued walking around the market and saw other interesting foods, including a few I could actually identify. Later that night we went out to a Korean restaurant, and I had another chance to sample a unique dish, *medahdahk*, which translates to "something that grows on rocks in the sea."

It looked like a small disc-shaped date, about the size of a quarter. Eating medahdahk was like trying to chew leather. It just wouldn't melt in my mouth. I kept chewing and chewing. Finally, I was able to get it down. Then there was another delicacy. It is called *keh* (crab), not to be confused with *keh* (dog). About the size of a half-dollar, there was no way to crack this item open and get the meat out. There was really only one way to eat it and that was to plop the entire crunchy crab in your mouth. Dipped in a spicy brown sauce, it was quite tasty and I went for seconds. We washed it down with a rich, milky brown liquid called bone soup.

My hosts smiled in delight.

Suddenly an image came to me from the show *Star Trek*. Many times, the captain for one reason or another had to eat food with aliens. Now I was at the Klingon table bravely eating greglock or gagh. There was the time when Commander Reicher was eating with a bunch of aliens. They handed him bondegi.

Reicher threw it in their faces and made his getaway. I am proud to say that I was much braver than Reicher. I had two helpings.

Bondegi is a throwback to a time when Koreans were so poor that they had to eat . . . well . . . worms. While many Koreans love the taste (it reminds them of their childhood) they are also a little embarrassed by it. That's why I claimed it was my favorite food. They were inevitably stunned.

"What? Bondegi! You like Bondegi?"

After I joined the university English department, the Korean faculty invited other English teachers to a fancy Korean restaurant in downtown Daegan. I couldn't resist saying "bondegi" when the dean asked me to name my favorite Korean food.

The Korean teachers all gasped, some of them even clapped. Seconds later another cheer rose up. I spun around and my jaw dropped open because the waiter arrived with a big steaming bowl of bondegi.

"Frank. You are so lucky. They have your favorite food. Here waiter, put it here in front of Frank. Now you can eat as much as you like. Smiling, with all eyes on me, I thought about Reicher and wondered what he would do. Then I slowly picked one up (making sure it was not still moving) and popped it in my mouth. They watched every crunch until I swallowed, smiled and asked for more. They were really proud of me. I picked up another and kept eating until I finished two-thirds of that bowl.

As we were finishing up, the dean leaned over and said, "Frank, you love that bondegi so much why don't you take it home. You can eat it for a snack before going to bed."

Looking For Foie Gras In All The Wrong Places

JULIA NIEBUHR EULENBERG

FRIENDS WITH AN APARTMENT IN PARIS invited me to join them there several years ago. Paris, even without my husband, was too tempting to pass up. When he said, "I think you should go," I started packing. With frequent flyer miles and a place to stay, all I'd have to pay for were food, museums and a few gifts. I was prepared to savour the experience.

Unfortunately, I soon discovered that my friends' way of living in Paris was different from mine. I like to eat out as often as possible—at home or away. I was content to eat breakfast at the apartment—cheese from the *fromagerie* and croissants, juice, and a latté from the *patisserie* below. After a long day of touring, I was even willing to make do with the occasional roasted chicken from the *boucherie* on the corner and vegetables from the open-air market a few blocks away. Going beyond that seemed like a waste of my time in Paris. Still, I found myself eating their way much of that first week.

12

We packed sandwiches for the trip to Versailles: good baguettes, sliced beef and cheese.

We bought vegetables and cheese from the street market for another light lunch. My hostess cooked. I made ratatouille one evening from the eggplant, zucchini, onions and tomatoes I had bought at the street market that morning. We ate one or two simple meals at nearby restaurants. I was eager to try others.

My hostess never claimed to be a good housekeeper. "Life," she once said, "is full of more interesting things to do. I'd rather sit at my potter's wheel than drag out the vacuum." Fair enough, I thought; I don't clean the house every day either. What I hadn't considered was how far her attitude might carry into the kitchen. Crumbs on counters and the floor are one thing. They're easily swept up or, more politely, ignored. Food left out on the counter for several days is something else entirely. Although I often leave dirty dishes from one meal to the next, I am scrupulous about putting away meats and perishable foods. Room-temperature food didn't bother my friend.

Was it the foie gras or the duck that played havoc with my second week in Paris? I blame it on the foie gras because this allows me to spread the blame beyond my friend's kitchen.

She had taken a liking to foie gras. I had learned to like liver—a good paté, several versions of chicken livers, including my own chopped liver, and beef or veal liver with fried onions. I had watched Martha Stewart construct what she called foie gras with gel on top, though it was really little more than a paté. What I had never experienced was foie gras, in the French style.

In this presentation, the chef placed the whole goose liver on a grill for a few moments before laying it gently on a waiting leaf of lettuce. The dark patina gave the impression that the liver had spent some time near the flame, but that was an illusion. Soft and still very pink on the inside, the liver seemed raw. I didn't like it and, I soon discovered, it didn't like me.

My friends had found a new restaurant—a little place "within walking distance." For the uninitiated, those who live abroad have a tendency to use the terms "within walking distance" or "just a few blocks away, perhaps five minutes," when speaking of anything within a mile or so. "La Petite Niche," not its real name, was six blocks from the apartment, a long walk in temperatures that hovered around 3.9 Celsius, or not much more than 39 degrees Fahrenheit.

The warmth of the restaurant as we stepped inside was a relief, and a warm appetizer seemed appealing. I followed my friend's lead. The foie gras arrived, barely steaming, its center a delicate pink, its exterior crisp and almost blackened. Perfect, I suppose the French would have said. I ate the crisp, cooked part and put down my fork. I'm embarrassed to say that I silently wished for a bottle of ketchup, my way of handling American-style liver and onions. My friend offered me the remaining crisp part of her portion and ate what was left on both plates. I should have learned my lesson at the restaurant, but I ate foie gras again.

My hosts had invited guests for dinner on Sunday. They urged me to spend the afternoon wandering around the city. I stopped off for onion soup and a buckwheat crêpe before going on to the Cluny Museum to see the tapestries of the lady and her unicorn. It was my first visit to the museum, and I spent a lot of time just looking at the tapestries and thinking about what I had learned about tapestries—their patterns, the story of the lady and the unicorn and the techniques involved in making tapestries.

I returned to the apartment tired but happy and prepared to be a good guest. Then dinner was served. A small plate was set in front of me. A piece of foie gras quivered on a leaf of lettuce. Once again, I ate around the edges and washed it down with Perrier. The main course was duck, always slightly heavy on the stomach. At the end of dinner, feeling slightly green, I excused myself. The other four looked at me with pity, said it must be jet lag, and sent me off while they continued with their evening.

Late that night, the foie gras began to take its toll. In Mexico, this is called Montezuma's revenge. Perhaps in France, it is what felled Napoleon. In any case, a trip that had started in good health rapidly headed downhill. It was several days before my host began to ply me with Immodium, without success. I missed the opera. I missed the trip to Chartres. I missed most of Paris. That whole last week, I never wandered far from a bathroom.

My great plans of eating out—and of the sightseeing I had expected to do during my last week in Paris—were foiled. Worse, I watched pieces of Sunday's dinner sit out on the counter until Wednesday. I began to wash my own dishes before and after I ate. My Seattle doctor and I conferred by phone. "Eat the BRAT diet," he said. "Don't eat anything but bananas, rice, applesauce and toast." Never mind "eating nothing else" in Paris. Just trying to eat the BRAT diet there is not as simple as one might think. Applesauce does not come in cans; I learned how to make it in the microwave, one apple at a time. Since there was no toaster in the apartment, I used the broiler to toast baguette halves. I despise bananas. My host was good enough to go out to find melons. "At least they'll replace your electrolytes," he said as he cut up the first Cavaillon melon.

The Immodium and the diet began to work, and I ventured out once again. I bought gifts at the boutique around the corner and cashed my Euro travelers checks. My friend and I had lunch in an Israeli-style restaurant in the Jewish section of the Marais, We even went out to dinner once. At last, that terrible week was over. That is no way to feel about leaving Paris, but all I wanted to do was go home. I packed, got to the airport for my early morning flight, and boarded the aircraft. However, it was foggy that morning in Paris, and French pilots do not fly when they cannot see. We sat on the runway, strapped into our seats, for two hours. I was given special dispensation for trips to the toilet.

By the time we landed in London, I had missed my flight to Seattle. There was an aircraft headed for Vancouver, BC, but I presented a particular problem. Never mind the stomach condition I was coping with at the moment, I required oxygen for long-distance flights. Air Canada refused to be responsible for me on the last leg from Vancouver to Seattle, since they couldn't supply oxygen at such short notice. Unfortunately, I forgot about the note from my doctor saying I could fly between London and Paris without oxygen. It would have sufficed, had I remembered it, but now we were at a standstill. The British Airwats customer service representative was very kind. He patted my arm and gave me vouchers for an overnight stay at the Heathrow Hilton and for dinner and breakfast.

I'd begun to feel better and made the mistake of eating beyond the BRAT diet. By mid-evening, it was clear I was going nowhere in the morning. My stomach had betrayed me once again. I phoned British Air, and we began another saga. I explained as carefully as possible that if I tried to fly—which they wanted me to do—they and I would be in great trouble.

"Perhaps you should see a doctor," he sighed. "I'll see what I can work out." His British accent was clipped, but I detected a stifled laugh on the other end of the phone.

I called the concierge, and she arranged for a doctor. A few hours later, a pleasant, rotund East Indian man arrived with a note clearing me to fly, a packet of electrolytes to bring my potassium levels back to normal, and a prescription bottle with what he deemed to be an adequate supply of codeine.

"This will help stop you up," he said, holding the small brown bottle toward me.

I looked at the label. "It's not in my name," I said, noting Mrs. Amina Arbi's name at the bottom. "U.S. Customs will have a fit."

"Well," he said, "I do not think so, and after all, I did not know your name, did I? This will do."

I nodded my head doubtfully, thanked him for his help, and called room service. Glasses of ginger ale, Coke, water, apple juice and an order of toast were on their way. I took one codeine tablet and drank a glassful of blackberry-flavored electrolytes. By morning I was tired, but ready to fly.

I still have enough codeine for another trip, and nearly all the electrolyte packages. The next time I go to Paris or London or anywhere else, I'll pack them in my travel kit. Will I ever eat foie gras again? I think not. I'll stick to my own chopped liver—well done, with a bit of glazed onion.

Feeling Crabby

Loretta Graziano Breuning

A HUGE ROACH CRAWLED OUT OF THE CORN FLAKES BOX. Should I tell the kids when they come down for their first breakfast in Mexico?

Serving roach-infested cereal is a desperate act for a mother. But I knew the mere mention of roaches would drive my kids to a hunger strike. I've spent so much time in the Third World that I don't expect the next box of cereal to be much better.

Probably the roach didn't touch the cereal, I rationalized, since the inner bag was shut.

Probably it was just a cicada.

I should feel guilty about bringing my son and his friends here under false pretenses. We were in a surfers' paradise, but they expected a resort, not a remote coastal village with dirt roads, feral dogs and indifferent sewer pipes. Another one of mom's "look-how-good-you-have-it" lessons sneaked into their vacation.

18

As I sat at the breakfast bar weighing the options, I saw something move. A speck the size and color of a grain of sand, but definitely moving. Then another speck, and soon it was clear that the beige Formica was swarming with tiny pale creatures that waddled like crabs.

We could always go out for breakfast. But if our kitchen was swarming, a restaurant would be, too. I thought of the previous night's restaurant outing.

"I want it."

"Give me some."

"Pass it here."

"What are you guys talking about?"

"Hand sanitizer."

Never in my travels through Haiti, Indonesia, Morocco, China or Egypt had I encountered hand sanitizer. But I stopped traveling after my son was born and progress continued. Having one's hygiene standards challenged by fifteen year-old boys is unsettling. I was forced to join their sanitation ritual. Then while eating my taco I unconsciously licked my fingers and gagged at the taste. There were more lessons to be learned here in Sayulita, Nayarit.

As the kids ran toward the kitchen, my maternal cost-benefit analysis resumed. I could just fess up. "No breakfast, kids. Our house has a roach. Yes, it is the most awful thing that has happened to mankind. Your mother is a bad person for bringing you to this four-bedroom beach house with dishwasher and VCR."

That would never work.

"Good morning, kids. The cereal seems stale. Why don't we finish the breakfast bars from the plane and have an early lunch."

The boys went surfing in an ocean full of squiggly-squirmy

things. Soon, a jellyfish stung one of them. Or maybe it was a sea urchin or a Portuguese man-of-war. The local surfers came to the rescue with a spray bottle of vinegar that helps soothe the sting. Have a friend pee on it if we're not around, they advised. This solution is attractive to teenage boys who never pass up an opportunity to display their first-aid skills.

When it became too dark to surf, the boys migrated to the swimming pool. I went to check on them and was stunned by an object hurtling into my face. It disappeared in an instant and then another swooped toward me. In pitch dark, bats could be seen swirling above the pool. No need to check on the kids any more, I decided. They swim better than me.

The next day we went to a bodega for snacks. I am no stranger to greasy food stalls and rat-infested produce markets. This shop was nice by my standards—it had a floor, a roof, no rotting stench and a few items in sanitary packaging. But the kids huddled outside and refused to enter. I found them cowering in front of blackened bananas lost in a cloud of fruit flies. Back at the house I chose their food and set up their lunch while they cleaned the lizard carcasses out of the pool. We ate amidst giant dragonflies.

There were a few moments each day when it was possible to forget the swarm. And there were nights when the bizarre gecko noise didn't disturb us because we mistook it for the rattle of a broken air conditioner.

On our last day, we had our picture taken for our hometown newspaper. The custom is to have yourself photographed reading a copy in an interesting foreign locale. We stood in front of the surfboard rental stand on the beach and asked the proprietor to snap our picture. He read the headline on the paper as we held it up—a report on our town's controversial dog-leash laws.

"They put dogs on leashes in America, Pepe!" he shrieked to the tiny Chihuahua near his foot. Working himself into a frenzy, he grabbed a rope and tied it to Pepe's neck. "This is what they'd do to you in America," he said, tugging lightly on the rope until Pepe began barking. Then he untied the dog, dramatically shouting "You're free, Pepe, you're free!" Pepe tottered off to join the lactating dogs milling on the sand. Thanks for your help, señor. Don't worry, we won't restrain your dogs, your jellyfish, your bats or your bugs. We celebrate their freedom.

By the last day of the trip, the kids were comfortable eating in local taquerias and ordering in Spanish. Then we confronted an exquisite bowl of homemade salsa. The kids with respectable mothers had been admonished not to eat raw vegetables, and in turn warned my son. Not me. I spent a year in Africa and marched to my own anthropologically correct drummer.

While packing for our departure, I came down with intestinal violence on an unprecedented scale and helped myself to the one antibiotic capsule I'd brought along. Just when all the pharmacies had closed for the day, my son also took ill and suffered all night long.

The next morning, after skipping breakfast, we said goodbye to the American lady who rented us the house, I asked, "What's it like here in the off season?"

"Sand crabs invade the house. It's not their fault. Their usual path from the beach is blocked by the new wall I built in the garden. Their only choice is to go through the living room."

Afterwhile Crocodile

Darla Kay Fitzpatrick

To be honest I never thought about the food when I agreed to volunteer at Mother Teresa's orphanage for disabled children in Lima. A local cook prepared all of my vegetarian meals at the volunteer house and the Peruvian cuisine embraced a long Hispanic culinary tradition. I felt comfortable and safe and never considered dining out.

Then a lecturer convinced me that a side trip into the Amazon Basin would broaden my understanding of this fascinating region. That was how I found myself in Iquitos, the largest jungle town in Peru, during my second week in South America. I hired a guide, Reynaldo, and climbed into his boat for a week on the muddy Amazon. Soaring birds, screeching monkeys, the damp smell of the fertile soil, torrential rains and brilliant sunsets made this a voyage of discovery. Born and raised in the jungle, Reynaldo was the perfect escort.

Farther down the Amazon, Reynaldo docked the boat and headed into the jungle armed with a machete. I followed until he noticed I was shaking and led me back to the riverbank. Convinced I was hungry, he started a fire, made a crude fishing pole and line, and began preparing our meal from the jungle. Through a combination of charades, English, and broken Spanish, I learned Reynaldo was a Ticuna Indian from Brazil, speaking Ticuna and Portuguese. His Spanish was as limited as my own. But when it was time to eat, our language barrier did not get in the way.

Reynaldo used his machete to cut a mango for my dinner along with fish, bananas and a number of unfamiliar entrees. I had been warned at the Lima volunteer house that some fish were toxic to foreigners. Reynaldo misunderstood my questions about this perceived problem. Within minutes he handed me a sharpened a long stick like his own and I was walking behind him in the knee-deep waters of the Amazon.

Reynaldo lunged so suddenly at the water with his stick that I nearly fell on top of him. I ran to the bank screaming as he lifted his stick to expose wriggling gray-green legs and a tail. He returned with dinner, lit a fire and then proceeded to skin, gut and cook the crocodile.

My first nonvegetarian dinner on the Amazon was superb, as were successive meals created from the jungle's bounty. Reynaldo and I ate bananas, mangoes, a roasted root and a catfish-type fish. The fruit was the freshest, juiciest and messiest I had ever eaten. The roasted root was rather bland, but filling and I enjoyed the mild white fish. The chewy crocodile was decent.

For the next ten days Reynaldo and I were rolling on the river, I learned that most anything edible, animal or vegetable, might be on the menu. No picky eaters allowed. I learned to fish for piranha, pick fresh fruit from the trees and tried hunting crocodile again without the special effects. The second croc was much tastier— and not nearly as tough. As a new hunter and gatherer I learned that a subsistence lifestyle is a good way to cut down on food bills. I also ate some of the freshest and healthiest food of my life.

I still have cravings for the tiny bananas that taste like caramels and for fresh mangoes and passion fruit impossible to find back home in Washington. I also learned there are times when vegetarians need to be flexible. And when it comes to fresh-caught crocodile, it's always a pleasure to be the consumer rather than the consumed.

BANQUET BLUES

ALEC LE SUEUR

from *The Hotel On The Roof Of The World*, © 2003 by Alec LeSueur

DURING THE MORNING MEETING OF 30 SEPTEMBER, Jig Me announced that the National Day banquet that Chef had been preparing for National Day, 1 October, would now be a day early because National Day was a public holiday. Heather translated into Chinese and the Tibetans and Hans smiled: a day off work. Mr. Pong rumbled in his chair, giving the expatriates time to push their seats back in anticipation of the tidal wave of halitosis that would engulf all around the table, but the general manager stopped him short: "You mean the banquet that we are preparing for tomorrow is now going to be today?"

"Yes," it was Jig Me who replied. "Today at seven p.m."

Although there was considerable relief that Mr. Pong had been kept silent, the confirmation that the National Day banquet was a day early had caught all the expatriates off guard. Chef had given his sous chefs the day off, the storerooms were empty and the local purchasing manager had not been

25

seen for three days. Nevertheless, in ten hours, the top VIPs of Lhasa would be arriving for the National Day banquet—the highest social event on the Lhasa calendar. The evening had to be a success. There could be no more embarrassments. The loss of face over the dismissal of Gunter was still fresh in everyone's mind, and we badly needed to restore the prestige image of the hotel and boost the morale of the expatriates.

Chef left immediately for the kitchens to check which extra provisions he would need for the evening. Tu Dian, the Tibetan deputy F&B manager, followed him.

"May-oh wenti!" Tu Dian called out as he left the room.

Translated literally as "no problem," *may-oh wenti* was always a worrying remark. With the laid-back attitude of the Tibetans, instead of meaning "no problem, we can solve this one" *may-oh wenti* usually meant "no problem—the evening will be a disaster."

Chef was determined that there would be no problems with the food that evening. He wanted to show that his side of the F&B Department could run just as well now that Gunter had left. He was particularly keen on giving a good impression for the general manager, as he was relying on a recommendation for a transfer to a less stressful part of Asia.

I passed Chef's office on my way back from the morning meeting, and caught a glimpse of him giving instructions to his staff. It was a surreal scene: 30 Chinese and Tibetans dressed in kitchen whites packed in a tiny office, staring with expressionless faces at a peculiar European flailing his arms about in the air. Although his Chinese vocabulary did not extend far beyond the essential phrases of *"mayoh," "putchidao"* and *"may-oh wenti,"* he had an exceptionally high level of understanding with his staff.

He had been without an interpreter for over a year and

had developed a form of kitchen sign language with which he could communicate perfectly with both Tu Dian and the cooks.

With the index and middle finger of his right hand he made jumping motions across the table, and with his left hand he made a series of mock karate chops over his knuckles. He nibbled his right index finger and made an imitation of steam blowing out of his ears. There was much discussion and nodding amongst the cooks who smiled in recognition of the dish—Sichuan frog legs with chili peppers.

The other VIP dish was harder to mime, but as it was always requested at the top banquets it was an easy one to guess. Chef pulled his head back and hunched up his shoulders to hide his neck. He brought up his hands, palms outermost, to the top level of his shoulders and waved his fingers at his cooks. This confirmed what they had expected—turtle would be served at the National Day banquet. Tu Dian rushed off into town with the market list. Dorje, the hotel driver, was waiting for him in one of the Holiday Inn Land Cruisers so there was no doubt that it would be the fastest shopping trip possible.

The general manager spent the afternoon putting the restaurant staff through their paces. The banquet would be in the form of a self-service buffet—the simplest Food & Beverage formula—where it would be difficult to make mistakes.

The idea of waitress service for a banquet of over 200 people had been abandoned. Even in the small coffee shop the a la carte service was a disaster. It was hardly the fault of the waitresses. They had never seen any world other than their own isolated land of Tibet and had no idea how a Western restaurant should work.

The most basic rules of restaurant service were totally

alien concepts to them. No matter how many times it was explained that the starter should be delivered before the main course, they invariably made the guests wait half an hour and then brought starter, main course and dessert in every conceivable order except for the correct one. All the permutations and combinations of dishes were tried out: main course first, soup next, dessert last; all at the same time; none at all; only the drinks and not the food; the starter for the adjacent table with a dessert that had never been ordered. The waitresses considered it to be of little importance, as long as the guest received his food he should be happy. Pointing out a mistake to the waitress was inadvisable whilst the meal was still in progress. This would lead to everything being grabbed from the table and rushed back into the kitchen. The same food would come out ten minutes later (and ten minutes cooler) and the waitress would try to remember who had been eating from which plate. It was very complicated.

A straightforward buffet for the National Day banquet was the safest bet for a trouble-free evening. All that the waitresses had to do was to set the tables, serve drinks and clear the tables afterwards. It seemed simple enough.

I was called into the banquet room late in the afternoon to check on the English lettering for a 40-foot-long, five-foot-wide banner that was being hoisted above the head table.

The giant white letters of 'NATIONALDAYRECETCION' beamed out across the room, pinned onto a background of bright red cloth. The only minor problem was that all the letters ran in a continuous line. There was some dismay when I asked for the words to be separated and for the spelling to be corrected. Chinese and Tibetan characters, presumably saying the same message, had already been glued across the top of the banner and there was no space left to split the lettering onto different lines. We eventually settled for the solution of squashing the letters closer together so that there was enough space to distinguish the individual words.

Beneath the banner, the long top table was being set for 20 Lhasa VIPs. Charlie had been persuaded to part with the only white tablecloths to be found in Lhasa on condition that he personally supervised the method of securing them to the table—an intricate valance of blue, red and gold brocade edged with red silk, hung around the front of the table.

The hotel's two silver candlesticks decorated with spirals of gilded dragons stood in the center, between the silver place settings for the vice-governor of Tibet, the consul general of Nepal and the head of the Foreign Affairs Office. The top table was fit for a king.

By a quarter to seven, the general manager could take five minutes to relax, confident that after spending the entire afternoon showing the waitresses how to clear tables and serve drinks, they would make a star performance. Tu Dian had found all the ingredients in the market, and Chef and his team had prepared a mouth-watering buffet. At least mouth-watering if, like the VIP guests, you take a fancy to lightly poached turtle in its own broth, tiny frogs legs that blow you away and Chinese hacked chicken, chopped into portions guaranteed to contain a greater percentage of minute bone splinters than edible meat. Fortunately, the banquet menu contained a few Western favorites: tenderized yak steaks, pork chops and mashed potato and a tasty dish of beef slices with green peppers.

Chef had even been able to find his best watermelon engraver in the staff quarters and had set him to work on a display for the buffet table. Minute sections of the dark green outer skin of the watermelons were carved away with the point of a kitchen knife, forming contrasting patterns with the paler green inside. Delicate pictures of cranes and Chinese ladies now turned the humble melons into temporary works of art.

The general manager made his last inspection of the banquet room at five to seven. He stopped at the centerpiece of the buffet: an enormous watermelon depicting rural scenes from mainland China. His eyes screwed into focus on a moving black cloud that hovered above melon.

His gaze followed into the center of the room and back to the buffet table.

"Flies!" he screamed out. "Where is Housekeeping? Where is Chef? Why do I have flies at the most important banquet of the year?!"

The waitresses disappeared and the cooks behind the buffet table made themselves busy. Derek, the chief engineer, arrived.

"Why are there no fly screens on the windows in this room?" the general manager bellowed at him. There was no table to thump as he was standing up.

"Well, I, err. You see the fly screens needed repair and my men have been very busy and well, we thought the banquet was tomorrow and err . . ."

"No. Don't answer me. Get me Housekeeping! Get me the spray!"

Charlie came puffing and panting into the banquet room with a box of aerosol cans. Chef rushed his food display back into the kitchen as the general manager tore the wrapping from the first can.

"If you want something done around here, who has to do it?" he muttered to himself as he fumbled with the cans in the box. Taking one can in each hand; he held his arms aloft and with his forefingers tightly on the spray buttons, marched down the gangways between the tables, showering the contents of the cans into the room.

The hosts for the evening, the Foreign Affairs Office of Tibet, arrived just as the last cans had been emptied. A cloud of insecticide hung across the room and the waitresses held napkins to their faces in an attempt to avoid inhaling the sickly spray.

"A very beautiful room," the chief of the Foreign Affairs Office remarked to the general manager through Mrs. Chen, the official interpreter, "and a very pleasant scent you have made in the room for us tonight."

"Yes, especially for you," the general manager bowed graciously in reply.

The chief of the Foreign Affairs Office thanked him profusely and set about forming a line of FAO personnel by the door to welcome the banquet guests. Arriving military commanders and Party chiefs were shown to their respective places along the head table. This always took some time as, if you are invited to sit at the head table, it is usual etiquette to feign, "Oh no, surely not me sitting at the head table!" and to insist on first taking a place at one of the normal round tables where the common masses, or proletariat, would be sitting. Only after several more pleadings from the hosts do you then proceed to the head table, still shaking your head in disbelief at the great honor bestowed upon you, and making loud protests that you are not worthy.

The general manager was dragged from behind the buffet table, where he had been inspecting the cooks' uniforms, and forced by the Foreign Affairs Office to sit at a position of honor towards one end of the head table.

It was no feigning when he pleaded not to sit there but

despite his protestations that he had to oversee the banquet, the hosts made it very clear that as head of the international hotel in town, he was to take a seat at the VIP table.

For the minor dignitaries and the other foreign residents; seating had been arranged by the Foreign Affairs Office at round tables. Each table was reserved for a particular work unit, which is the comradely phrase used by the Chinese to describe any entity which provides employment. Table six, where I was sitting with the expatriates from the hotel work unit, was in the furthest corner of the room, pressed tight into the right-angle formed by the wall and the line of windows behind the head table. A loudspeaker stood as high as my chair, just behind me in the angle of the corner.

I should have thought ahead to what this would mean but at the time I was too busy being introduced to our hosts to realize the significance of this unfortunate seating position.

At our table was one of the deputy directors of the Foreign Affairs Office, his translator and several people whose jobs the translator couldn't translate. The translator, a young girl in her early twenties with a Tibetan mother and a Han-Chinese father, had recently returned from the Foreign Affairs School in Beijing, where she had been taught "diplomatic English." This is a clever type of language that involves talking constantly to diplomats without telling them anything at all.

The National Day banquet was her first official function and as a deputy director of the Foreign Affairs Office was sitting at our table, she was especially anxious to ensure that all the foreigners at table six were having a good time.

She smiled nervously at everyone.

"Please enjoy yourselves. Help yourself. Please enjoy yourselves," she repeated incessantly, with the frequency of worn-out vinyl.

Spilling over one of the chairs at our table was a rotund Tibetan whom I had not met before. He wore a Western suit with an assortment of stains down the front, an unbuttoned shirt and a wrongly knotted polyester tie. He looked most uncomfortable. He sat silent, scowling through most of the party, but his whole face lit up whenever anyone spoke to him. Our translator introduced him as a "living Buddha" and head of the Tibetan Buddhist Association. I suppose that being a living Buddha himself, he would be the right person for the job. He did once break a long silence in conversation around the table by proposing a toast to everyone for their hard work. He knocked back a glass of Lasa Beer and, apart from a further statement that the hotel should have more Tibetan decoration, he remained more or less silent to the very end. He was by the far the most interesting person at our table and I wished that I spoke Tibetan, so that I could have learnt more from him, rather than just exchanging pleasantries through the stilted words of our jittery "please enjoy yourselves" translator.

Sitting at table eight were the Germans from the Lhasa Leather Factory. Chancellor Kohl had promised German support for a Tibetan project during his visit to Lhasa in 1987, and this unlikely business enterprise was the result.

Three German technicians and their wives battled against the odds to produce high-quality leather products from Tibetan yak skins. It was an uphill struggle. Most of their work went into producing shoes and jackets for local use, but a small outlet in the hotel provided some foreign exchange from selling yak-skin trinkets to eager tourists.

They had lived for a while in the hotel, before their own accommodation had been built at the leather factory on the outskirts of the city near the new army barracks. Closer to the hotel were the expatriates of the two Lhasa-based charity projects, or 'NGOs' (Non-Governmental Organizations) as they like to be called. Save the Children Fund from Britain and Médecins Sans Frontières from Belgium maintained highly active offices near the city center. The numbers of foreigners working there varied according to project needs, but usually consisted of a small community of between five and ten staff from Britain, Holland, Belgium and France. The Swiss Red Cross was the only other NGO based in Tibet but their headquarters were in Shigatse, some 200 miles to the west. Unbelievable as it seemed to some of the hotel expatriates, who considered that there could be no town on earth more primitive than Lhasa, the Swiss couple stationed in Shigatse regularly came on trips to Lhasa to see the big city of bright lights and shops.

Overworked and under-funded, the three NGOs were stretched to the limits to push ahead with their Tibetan projects. Village schools were built, TB inoculations given out by the bucketful, local doctors were trained and wells were sunk in waterless villages. It was a rare example of aid organizations working together in providing meaningful help to the local population.

It was a stark contrast to the aid effort in neighboring Nepal, from where stories regularly drifted up about the immense bungling of foreign aid projects. The entire economy of Nepal depends on overseas aid and the opportunities for corruption and mismanagement on a large scale are enormous.

We occasionally saw the effects of foreign do-gooder organizations in Tibet, who would sail through, handing out wads of money and Toyota Land Cruisers to the first who asked. The only effect this had on the local population was that certain minor officials suddenly had enormous amounts of spending money and some very nice cars to go shopping with.

The expatriates of the NGOs in Tibet were frequently in the

hotel, meeting diplomats who were looking for suitable causes to give foreign aid to. They looked forward to the charade of the National Day celebrations about as much as we did.

The only foreigners who really enjoyed the banquet were the English teachers. Six Americans lived downtown in the harshest conditions of any foreigners in Tibet, teaching English for practically no salary except meager pocket money and biannual airfares to Hong Kong.

They were a peculiar mix of people. Some were genuine teachers with a taste for adventure but others had ulterior motives. It did not take long to distinguish the real ones from the fakes: their uniforms gave it away. You know those people who knock on your door and ask you if you've read Revelations recently? Have you ever wondered what they wear when they don't have suits and briefcases? Well the answer is dungarees and lumberjack shirts. Some of the so-called teachers had entire wardrobes of dungarees and lumberjack shirts, sported suspiciously sensible haircuts and smiled intensely at everyone in sight. A real giveaway.

At the table nearest the door was a group of foreigners whom I was sure I had not seen in Lhasa before. It would have been hard to miss them. They wore a selection of dark purple corduroy jackets with flapping lapels over butterfly collars on nylon shirts. Flared drip-dry trousers of the non-crease variety draped over dirty training shoes.

Their flat hairstyles, sticking to the sides of their faces over long side burns, gave telltale signs that they used the same shampoo as Heather and with the same frequency.

But large bushy moustaches and round European eyes ended the similarity. I asked our translator who they were.

"Please enjoy yourselves. We warmly welcome you," she twitched at me for an answer.

I found out later, from Harry (who had also made enquiries), that they were six Romanians who had set up a beer factory in Lhasa, as an overseas aid project of the Romanian government. They were living on the factory site, beneath Sera monastery, and were about to return to Romania, having just completed the installation of the bottling plant. Green 70 cl beer bottles were imported from China, together with the hops and the machinery. Tibet provided most of the labor force and the water. It was another great leap forward in the modernization of Tibet, this time with help from their modern Romanian comrades.

The words "Lasa Beer" appeared on the label, with writing in Tibetan and Chinese, surrounded by two jumping fish—an auspicious Tibetan symbol. This led to many a suggestion about the contents but despite the flavor varying from bottle to bottle, the beer sold well, particularly to Khampas. It was predominantly watery, sometimes with a hint of a noxious chemical, perhaps a detergent concentrate, and occasionally it was so strong that it knocked you off the kebab stand. We tended to drink it with the excuse that we were supporting the local economy, and all the expatriates at table six requested a Lasa Beer from the waitress who came to take our drinks order.

Suddenly, there was an ear-piercing screech in the banquet room. The loudspeaker behind my chair had leapt off the floor as Mrs. Chen shrieked into her microphone.

We all turned to Derek, the chief engineer. He always needed a push to get him into action and had a store of unimaginative excuses for not being able to do things.

"There's nothing wrong with it!" he shouted across the table. As Derek was hard of hearing from working most of his life in ships' boiler rooms it was no surprise that he found the noise level bearable. However, the rest of us had no intention of spending the evening sitting inches away from the interpreter's amplified squawks, so he reluctantly agreed to adjust the volume. Derek waved to one of his Engineering Department staff, who was standing by the doorway in the opposite corner of the room. He pointed to the loudspeaker and made a turning motion with his hand to indicate that the volume needed to be lowered.

The man in the Engineering Department uniform waved back to Derek, nodded and ran out of the door.

Derek, who liked to tell anyone who had the misfortune to be stuck in one of his monologue conversations, that all of his staff understood him perfectly, was somewhat put out by this. "He must have gone to get something," he stammered.

The volume remained at full blast.

Mrs. Chen, a Han-Chinese lady from the Foreign Affairs Office who they wheeled out every year for the occasion, continued her preamble to the top table introductions, unaware of the decibel level at table six. She used the standard Chinglish phrases for official parties: "We warmly welcome all our guests. We warmly welcome you to enjoy yourselves. We warmly welcome you to celebrate."

Her peculiar pronunciation and an unfortunate lisp, led to the "Tibet Autonomous Region of China" becoming the "Tibet Anonymous Region of China," and this curious turn of speech, interspersed with "we warmly welcome you to your comings" was well received by the foreigners.

Derek was relieved when the engineer he had sent to turn the volume down reappeared by our table. "You see," he shouted, "I don't need to speak Chinese, these people understand me."

The man from the Engineering Department handed him a microphone, a length of electrical cable and a spare plug socket. "No, no, that's not what I wanted. Noise. Down. Turn it down!" He pointed to the loudspeaker. A waitress approached our table, straining under the weight of a tray fully laden with Lasa Beer bottles. Seeing the commotion where Derek was sitting, she carefully made her way around the back of the table, concentrating on keeping the tray steady just as the general manager had shown her.

Stepping forward to lower the tray onto the table, her left foot came down squarely on the electrical cable that led to the loudspeaker. A noise similar to the crackle of gunfire shot from the sound system as the plug snapped out of its socket and our loudspeaker was silenced.

It was too late for Derek to stop the words coming out of his mouth. His exclamation of "TURN IT DOWN!" coincided precisely with the moment of silence created by the unplugging of the loudspeaker and a pause in the introductions from Mrs. Chen. All heads, including the vice-governor's, turned to our table and a mortified chief engineer shrank in his chair. The military commanders glanced over their shoulders and the general manager kept a fixed angry stare at our table.

"Please enjoy yourselves," our translator continued, as if nothing had happened. The living Buddha smiled, and the startled waitress poured out Lasa Beers as the head table introductions resumed.

Mrs. Chen read out the name of each of the guests at the head table, and the VIP stood up to return a polite clap to the applauding crowd. The situation was complicated by the audience not knowing whether to applaud after the Chinese introduction or after the English introduction.

The interpreter didn't know whether to wait for applause and then translate, or translate and then hope the applause would follow. The result was a table-load of embarrassed VIPs who received a constant trickle of feeble applause, rendering it impossible to hear exactly what each of their titles was. Snippets of translation could occasionally be made out over the din: "The deputy chairman of the Standing Committee for Internal Affairs of the Tibet Anonymous Region . . . Please warmly welcome the coming of the vice-chairman of the Political Bureau of the Party of the Tibet Anonymous Region . . ."

When the introductions were over, the speeches began. They were always terrific. A copy in English would be circulated to the foreigners present so that we didn't have to rely on the spoken words of the interpreter to understand the wonderful statements being made. Chinglish, the Pidgin English version of Chinese and English combined, is funny enough as a language but Communist Chinglish is an art form in its own right. It is an extraordinary language that ignores negatives, conveniently forgets atrocities and speaks only of good things. Figures, particularly exceeded quotas and increased production percentages, are scattered liberally throughout Communist Chinglish to add scientific weight to the language and to prove beyond all doubt that the truth is being told. Mastering this language is even more important than learning Mandarin Chinese for the foreigner who wants to succeed in China. Who would have thought of calling the armed invasion of Tibet the "peaceful liberation," or describing the gunning down of innocent Tibetans in the Barkhor as "winning great victory against the splittists in the anti-split struggle?"

No one dares to laugh out loud and the Chinese and Tibetans all nod their heads in agreement with what is being said. They do not even listen to the words. The speeches are always the same and, as they are not permitted to disagree with what is being said, it is better just to sit there quietly and go along with whatever the speech writers are saying.

The most powerful politician in Tibet, Mr. Mao Ru Bai—the vice-governor—took the stage to deliver the National Day message. Mao Ru Bai was an articulate speaker and had the baby-kissing appearance that would even have made him a successful politician—if voting had been necessary to be in power. His receding hairline and permanently shining forehead gave him an unusually distinguished appearance compared with his political peers, who always looked as if they had just come off the back of a yak. He smiled continually and oozed understanding and compassion, even when uttering harsh words about the splittists. He gave short bursts of speech and glancing across at Mrs. Chen, twitched his cheekbones while pausing for her to translate.

The start of the speech never altered: "Cordial greetings to all the workers, peasants, herdsmen, intellectuals, cadres, soldiers and to Tibetans residing abroad."

In fact, pretty much, "a big hello to everyone." The main part of the speech would deal with the great leaps forward against the "splittists," regardless of how recently the last riots took place, and would highlight all the wonderful changes that had occurred since the Chinese had taken over in Tibet. The Cultural Revolution and the destruction of over 6,000 monasteries were temporarily overlooked. No mention was ever made as to whether new fire extinguishers had been ordered for the police station.

There were also some warnings for Western spectators. The 1991 speech contained this frightening sentence concerning the movements of the Chinese: "Strong socialist China now erects like a giant in the east of the world."

Some interesting facts concerning Chinese policies in Tibet were also revealed: "Since the peaceful liberation, under the correct leadership and kind attention of the central committee and state council (oops, they forgot to mention the Cultural Revolution here) we have scored great victory of democratic reform, and established a new political power—the people's democratic dictatorship."

The speech following the National Day message is always read by the Nepalese consul general. He speaks in English, but his Nepalese accent is so strong that little of what he says in intelligible. Luckily, the wording of the speech follows the same format as Communist Chinglish, so that the interpreter is able to understand and all the Tibetans and Chinese nod in agreement with whatever it is that he is saying.

The speech runs around the monotonous theme of the good cooperation between the two great countries. It is true that it has been a long time since Kukri-wielding Gurkhas invaded Tibet, but even Chinese speechwriters would have a hard time describing the Nepalese excursions into Tibet as entirely peaceful and the Nepalese consul general carefully avoided the subject.

It was after 47 minutes of speeches, with the boredom threshold long surpassed, that the flies started to drop out of the sky. The fly spray had been used in such quantities that not a single diptera in the room had a chance of survival.

Chef paced up and down his buffet, pinching them out as they landed. The Nepalese consul general droned on in the background as we watched the first fly crash-land on table six. It had landed on the rim of the living Buddha's glass of Lasa Beer and teetered dangerously from side to side. We watched it in eager anticipation: it was 50:50 as to whether it would fall into the glass or onto the table.

"Ten yuan the glass," whispered Harry.

"Ten yuan the table," Derek replied.

The fly carried on its walk around the rim. Harry tugged the tablecloth. With one final rub of its front legs it stood back and dropped straight into the glass. The living Buddha was unperturbed. He pulled it out with his finger and placed it gently on his napkin where it would dry out. The next fly to hit the table, made an impressive spiral nosedive, landing directly in front of our translator, who pretended to ignore it. But this one was closely followed by an entire squadron of the innocent insects, who bumped noiselessly onto the table in their last seconds of life.

Beyond boredom is that dangerous zone where your eyelids take over control of your body. Regardless of the message from your brain that this is not the right place or time to fall asleep, your eyelids close and your head lolls forwards. You only realize this has happened when you jerk your head back, opening your eyes wide and staring out at the person opposite you. But even the intense embarrassment is not enough to save you from your eyelids taking control again and your head drooping forwards.

Several at table six had entered this zone when Mrs. Chen shrieked into her microphone to announce that the Nepalese consul had finished his speech and that we would shortly be warmly welcomed to start the buffet.

The guests of the head table and the tables nearest the door set off first and a queue 30 feet long and three people deep formed across the center of the room. Unfortunately the person at the head of the queue had not realized that you should start a buffet from one end and then move along it, from the hors d'oeuvres, soups, main course, through to the desserts. Instead, he had walked to the middle of the long

42

buffet table and was now at a loss as to whether to turn left for the main courses, or right for the starters. The rest of the queue had to follow him and soon the congestion at the buffet table became chaotic, with hungry banquet guests going both ways, colliding as they attempted to cross the large queue, which now firmly blocked off the middle section.

Our table six translator was still saying "Please help yourselves, please enjoy yourselves, warmly welcome you to enjoy yourselves," and the living Buddha was going through one of his long silent phases, when we were warmly welcomed to enjoy the buffet and asked to join the queue into the melee. The military commanders were already pushing their way back through the line, with plates piled high in triumph, as we joined the end of the queue.

There are many deep-rooted misconceptions between Chinese and Westerners but none deeper than the Chinese idea of how to tackle a Western buffet. Some mischievous Westerner has told the Chinese that there are special rules to follow when attending a Western buffet and these rules are now taken to be unbreakable:

1. You are to use one plate only. A bowl is optional for soup but only if it can be carried at the same time as the one plate used for the buffet.

2. You are allowed one visit only to the buffet table and on no account are you permitted to return.

3. You must absolutely stuff yourself but only in accordance with the limitations of rules 1 and 2.

With these false rules firmly implanted in the minds of everyone who attends a Western buffet, the lineup at the buffet table becomes a competition to see who can load up his plate highest. As we stood in the queue we watched Mr. Pong (from a safe distance) make his way along the buffet table.

He was an expert at Western buffets and had broken out of the T formation that was stuck in the middle of the table and moved along to the beginning of the hors d'oeuvres to stock up his plate. First, a few slices of imported cold meats and tomato salad. Next a bowl of turtle broth and a slice of bread balanced on the plate. He made room for a spoon from each of the hot dishes: a scoop of spicy aubergine, a pile of frogs' legs, a dollop of mashed potato, a pork chop, a spoon of hacked chicken splinters, sliced beef with pepper, a yak steak—just enough space for an extra scoop of frogs' legs, some cabbage, a piece of cauliflower and just a bit more room on top of the pile for two croquette potatoes. The dessert was always the trickiest part and showed the experienced Western buffet diner from the beginner. Mr. Pong expertly balanced a large slice of sponge cake on top of the flattened peaks of mashed potato and smothered it with a generous helping of yak yogurt. A black banana was curled around the rim of the plate and, content that he could fit no more on top, he negotiated his way through the crowd back to his table.

Eating from the mountain of food on the plate is interrupted periodically by a very Chinese custom that is as alien to us as buffet dining is to them. It is the custom of *gambay,* which can be translated as "bottoms up." Banquet drinking is a serious business and revolves around a particular alcohol called Mao Tai. Every few minutes someone at your table will suddenly blurt out "gambay," and everyone at the table has to stop whatever they are doing and drink a small glass of Mao Tai. It is one of the most insidious drinks known to mankind, and although they claim that the deceptively colorless liquid is a rice wine, it has a smell and a taste that bears a striking similarity to distilled cow dung—or at least to what you would expect distilled cow dung to taste like. If you hold your breath and swallow the tiny glassful in one go, you are spared the foul taste and only feel the burning sensation as it slowly dissolves your intestinal tract. It is incredibly powerful and can render the most solidly built person incoherently drunk within minutes.

Unfortunately, banquet drinking is a matter of honor and no one is allowed to escape. A refusal is a sign of weakness and a loss of face for the work unit. As few can drink much of this toxin without being seriously ill, cheating is rife. A common trick is to keep the Mao Tai in your mouth, pretend to wash it down with a drink of something harmless such as orange juice but when the glass of orange juice is at your lips you discreetly spit the Mao Tai into the orange. This has the disadvantage that your glass of orange fills up over the evening, which is a bit of a give away, and it also means that you taste the vile liquid while it is in your mouth. The best way of cheating is to fill your Mao Tai glass with water. This is a very common practice and if you are challenged to a *gambay* by someone approaching you with a glass, it is more than likely that they will have filled it up with water before coming over to your table.

Cheating goes to the extent of bribing waitresses to fill personal Mao Tai bottles with water so that the other party guests will see your glass being poured from the bottle and will believe it is the real thing. I once saw an entire table cheat by pouring Sprite into their Mao Tai glasses.

They would have got away with it, but the bubbles in the Sprite would not go away and they had to tap the glasses continuously on the table in an effort to dislodge them.

Cheating is a risky business, and those caught in the act bring disgrace to their unit and must pay the heavy price of drinking at least one full glass of the authenticated liquid.

The real Mao Tai comes from a small village in the south of China and, as with wine from the Champagne district of France, labeling is strictly controlled. There are many fakes and imitations, and the Mao Tai connoisseur can apparently tell the difference between the real cow-dung distillate and its imitators.

Considering that one bottle of Mao Tai costs twice as much as a worker earns in a week, banquet drinking is also an extremely expensive pastime. Fortunately, none of the individuals have to pay for the excesses, as it is always the work unit that hosts the banquets.

The use of Mao Tai for official banquets had been curtailed by the Beijing government in one of their major austerity drives. It was calculated that if every government banquet were to reduce the amount of Mao Tai drunk, a saving of millions of yuan could be made. But as Lhasa is an Autonomous region, the officials turned a blind eye to the Beijing rules. Judging by the amount of Mao Tai consumed at the National Day banquet, they would soon be turning a blind eye to everything.

Although Westerners find the *gambay* custom extremely difficult to follow, it has been easy for the Tibetans to adapt to this particular whim of the Chinese. According to Tibetan tradition it is very impolite to leave a party without showing the host that you are drunk.

Fortunately, the National Day Banquet does not linger on all night and the *gambays* come to an end as abruptly as they started. Shortly after the last frog's leg has been chewed and the mountain on the plate reduced to a pile of bone and debris spat out onto the table and the floor, the VIP guests thank everyone for a wonderful evening and then make a quick exit. Within a matter of minutes the rest of the room empties. There is no question of staying on with coffee, petit fours and liqueurs, and no one is asking for any more Mao Tai. Conversation amongst the expatriates is left to how well we cheated with the *gambays*.

"I had fourteen," Charlie chuckled, "only three real ones!"

Derek was not so lucky. He had been caught cheating and had been forced to drink the real thing. It was just as well there would be a day off work on National Day.

Congo Breakfast at Tiffany's

Scott Loveridge

As a Peace Corps Volunteer posted to Africa in Congo's bush country, I always found meals were an adventure. During the rainy season, the roads were deep-rutted slippery red clay. In the dry season, some areas were deep sand, while others produced clouds of red dust that choked lungs and machinery. There were also "security check points" every few miles, where underpaid soldiers would ask truckers to pay a bribe to be allowed to continue their journey.

I lived in one of the poorer parts of the vast nation, so not many people in my region could afford to buy processed or canned food expensively transported over those horrible roads. The closest grocery store was in a Kikwit, a few miles from my village. Most of the store's shelves were bare. Kikwit had electricity for only an hour or two a day, so purchase of fresh meat was impossible. I gradually accepted the fact that I would consume eggs for breakfast and beans for dinner . . . every day for the rest of my two-year assignment. The egg supply was reliable because my hens each produced an egg or two each day. But it was pretty boring eating the same thing for breakfast and dinner day after day.

I traveled to remote villages on foot or motorcycle to visit farmers for my work, so the noon meal was whatever the friendly villagers chose to offer—sometimes nothing, but usually cold foo-foo, a starchy food made from cassava flour and water. Foo-foo tastes a little like mashed potatoes, but with the consistency of modeling clay. To give the foo-foo a little flavor, my hosts often served it with a side dish of pounded leaves. On a good day, there might be fresh chicken. My Peace Corps training had told me that I had to eat whatever was served or risk offending the host. There might be what we called "bush meat" in the pot. Bush meat came from a variety of exotic critters such as antelope, pangolin, field rats, grubs or large caterpillars. On a bad day there might be meat that had been sitting in a pot, unrefrigerated, for a few days.

When an opportunity arose to go for training to Mbuji Mai, a big city in the wealthier diamond-producing part of the country, I looked forward to finding a good European-style meal. Travel to the Mbuji Mai diamond country was an adventure in itself, with a 4 A.M. departure, slow buses and a delayed flight. Roadside fare in Congo was limited to greasy doughnuts without the sugar. Missing a few meals would simply enhance the pleasure of my Mbuii Mai feast.

At the end of the conference's first evening, I was very hungry, and happy to join a large group of Peace Corps volunteers headed for a fancy local restaurant here in the diamond district. The menu posted in the window promised a full range of selections: steaks, pastas, fish and other delights. Although the prices listed on the menu were higher than we could really afford, this would be a memorable splurge I could look back on when I returned to foo-foo in the bush. My compatriots congratulated one another on finding this culinary oasis.

The maitre d'hotel greeted us, and we followed him through the carpeted, well-lit dining area to our table, which sported a clean white tablecloth, a full set of dishes and silverware at each place, and an artistically folded cloth napkin in the center of each plate. I was in heaven . . . a real restaurant!

The waiter, formally attired in a dark suit, approached to take our drink orders. This being Congo, with its perpetual shortages, I asked which items were available that night. The waiter recoiled. He appeared offended. "Sir, you only have to look at the menu and make your choice!" Ah, the magic of diamond country. Here, restaurants could obtain their ingredients! My group ordered drinks and happily began selecting dinner items from the book-sized menus.

A few minutes later, the waiter reappeared with our drinks. "Are you ready to order?" Yes, indeed, we were ready to order the first European-style food any of us had seen in months. A young woman on my left chose the pork cutlets. "Madame, I'm sorry but we have no pork cutlets tonight."

She re-examined the menu while the person next to her ordered. "Sir, I'm sorry we have no shish kebobs tonight."

This continued until the waiter had circumnavigated the table. None of our choices were available. We asked for more time. The waiter disappeared and returned a few minutes later. Again we went around the table, and again, none of the chosen items were available.

"What can you suggest tonight?" I asked.

The waiter smiled. "Sir, we are offering plain omelets without cheese." "Anything else?" "No sir, just omelets."

Like Holly Golightly we had found breakfast at Tiffany's, Congo style.

In Search of Mongolian Pie

LARRY JER

"Just sit right back and you'll hear a tale,
A tale of a fateful trip . . ."

THE LYRICS STRETCHED OUT ACROSS THE GRASSLANDS, powered by alcohol and punctuated by the tortured wail of the family watchdog. Everyone's a critic. We sang for our dinner: a feast of lamb, slain by our host, spiced and simmered in a cauldron over coals, served in washbasin buckets. Life was good.

We five had come to Inner Mongolia belting out the Gilligan's Island theme song in search of Mongolian Pie: An American, an Englishman and me, a Canadian, joining two Chinese ladies for a day trip.

We worked in Shenyang, northeast China, all teachers, but at different locations and at various points in our tenure. Ben, from Wisconsin, and Robert, of Oxford, had been in China about one year, and I was the grand old man, hailing from Vancouver, coming to the end of my two-year hitch. The ladies lived in the industrial city. We became friends through a potpourri of circumstances, but one thread that wove its way through our personalities was the desire to eat the varied foods of the region.

This latest episode started when my colleague, a Chinese teacher, asked if I had eaten Mongolian Pie. Her boyfriend raved about it, so she suggested we gather some friends and travel to Huolinguole, an Inner Mongolian town about eight hours by train northwest of our home city and track some down.

It was fun.

We made some fast friends in Huolinguole, the way you know foreigners can if you've ever traveled in China. A Mr. Wong chauffeured our group into the vast grasslands, where we stopped to chat with a few Mongolian families.

Through nods and smiles, the patriarch of one clan suggested I hop on one of his horses so we could go rope dinner, an unsuspecting lamb quietly grazing with the rest of the family's flock. I declined. In Vancouver's inner city, chasing dinner on horseback wasn't taught in public schools.

We stayed for hours, exchanging songs when conversation faltered. The day was full of goodwill and when we finally said our goodbyes, the entire group buzzed from the connection.

We made our way back to the train station where our bags had been stored. Our contentment was short-lived.

The police met us with some bad news: We were traveling in a "restricted" military area. Our bags were held ransom and, through a mishmash of English and Chinese, we were told we must pay a fine or be arrested. It was just a matter of how much or for how long.

Nice business the local gendarmerie ran.

They changed the rules or set them as they pleased. Prospecting for Mongolian Pie would cost us. For each foreigner, it was 5,000 yuan ($625), the cost of a ski weekend in, say, Utah, but several months' wages in China.

We refused to pay and were put under "house arrest," sequestered in the local hotel and forced to cough up for the "best" rooms. My four-star had no working lights, a backed-up toilet and cockroach carcasses in a few of the darker crannies.

We didn't take the detention seriously, even less so when ordered to write a self-criticism. Robert wrote in Latin (who said it was a dead language?), and I submitted an essay on what we had for lunch that day. Ben wrote bawdy lyrics to a rugby song. We knew the translator's English was lacking and that he probably had, like so many others in these positions, secured his job through nepotism—ill qualified for the task. He put up a decent front, staring in great concentration at the sheets of paper, nodded knowingly at appropriate intervals and ceremoniously discarding the self-criticisms one by one. One speed bump over and done with.

We had two choices for dinner: 1. Have one, or 2. Don't have one. We chose option 1 thinking what the hell, maybe we'll finally get some Mongolian Pie since it hadn't been on the menu at our meal with the clan. Official pumping of our pockets of cash continued, as Y25 each was charged. Dinner bell at six.

Y25 could easily have paid for all of us at any local restaurant, but that wasn't the kick. When we arrived promptly for dinner, the police were sitting at a huge, round table having a banquet, laughing raucously, red-faced from drinking. They were having a good time at our expense.

Between swigs of baijiu, the costliest alcohol in China, we

were told that due to our tardiness, they had to eat the meal as our treat. We went back to our respective rooms to stew overnight, hungry and angry.

I fell asleep listening to the party extend into the night. As day broke, I noticed my room faced a fenced courtyard where there was an enormous sow wallowing in the makeshift pen.

I thought at first it was a half-buried VW Beetle, but when it suddenly got agitated, I was surprised at how agile it could be.

The source of stress? The well-fed police had decided to-day was the day the giant pig was to be sacrificed and divided up for their families. Through my window, it was a one-channel horror film. At once the cops were adept at graft and blackmail and with the flip of a new day they were in gumboots and aprons pig-wrestling.

We gathered before the next tribunal. Robert had read in a guidebook that though this sticky situation happens on occasion, don't get flustered, negotiate a fee that satisfies all, and within a few hours you will be free to move on, your wallet thinner, your load generously lightened by a small Huolinguole hospitality surcharge. Ben wouldn't have any of that. He put in an anxious call to the American Consulate, but the cold voice on the other end did nothing to quell our concerns. "Let us know if they move you." Click.

More ideas were tossed around. The best brainchild was, "Just tell them we don't have the money and that we'll pay off our time in prison," knowing full well that the Chinese wouldn't send foreigners to jail.

If nothing else, we gave the police a stitch from laughing too hard.

"Don't have the money?" the cops questioned. "Prison?"

Grins widening fast. "We'll put the women in jail and escort one of you to Shenyang to get the money you owe."

Forty-eight hours of cat-and-mouse negotiations later and the matter was decided. Their ace was the simple mantra: "The longer we stay, the better food they will eat at our expense."

The cost for our adventure? Two days of bloated hotel fees, meals we paid for but didn't eat, limited and monitored movement, having to watch a giant pig's demise, a fine that plummeted from the astronomical Y5,000 down to an irritating Y140 (17 USD) but worst of all—still no Mongolian Pie.

Food Fight

Marius Bosc

Returning from France to San Francisco, my wife, Joyce, and I stopped in New York to see friends. One evening we decided to treat ourselves by going to a Chinese restaurant on the Lower East Side.

When Joyce and I arrived the place was full, which seemed to be a pretty good endorsement. After our food arrived, I tried my lo mein and didn't particularly care for the taste of the noodles, so I called our waiter over and told him so. To my astonishment, he replied that if I didn't like the food to "leave." I thought that rather odd, but replied "no" and figured I would wait for the others at our table to finish their meals. All of a sudden, the waiter came over and slapped me across the chest. I was surprised, but not too much to return the favor and slap him back.

Then all hell broke loose. He grabbed the chair, with me still in it, and swung it so that I went twirling across the room like a ballet dancer. Like an old Western saloon movie scene, people got up screaming and ran out of the restaurant while four or five waiters came at me with their fists.

After my arms gave out trying to fight back, I was knocked to the floor, where I was surrounded and kicked as I lay on my back and tried my best to fend off the blows. Finally, I took refuge underneath a pile of tables, only to look up and see a young waiter with a pistol pointed at my head.

I kicked away the gun, and at that point, to my ultimate relief, the police came and broke up the melee. Joyce and I were taken to the local precinct, where we found the waiters, chef, owner and his lawyers on one side of the room slowly filling out forms for court. It was only at that point that someone asked if they could take me to a hospital to check out my injuries, and so we went, under armed guard.

The adventure didn't stop there. When the nurse prepared to give me a tetanus shot, I told her I was allergic to some types of medication. She scoffed and called me a "big baby," while the man on the table next to me was heaving.

I survived the hospital to return to the precinct, where a policeman told me I'd have to go to court in a month. Explaining I was a visitor from San Francisco, I asked if I could just drop the charges. His answer: No, because he'd spent the last hour typing out the complaints.

What to do? I took matters into my own hands, went across the room and told the restaurant owner I would drop the charges if he would. The entire restaurant party looked relieved, including the waiter whose hand I had kicked, which now was the size of a small melon.

The owner and I shook hands, dropped the charges and we all left. On the way out, the owner slipped me some money. The next time I returned to New York, I noticed that the restaurant was boarded up.

PASS THE ANTEATER, PLEASE

CLAUDIA R. CAPOS

FOR MANY TRAVELERS IN AMERICA, Thanksgiving Day is fairly predictable. Ham or turkey with the relatives, followed by family chitchat or football games on TV. But not for me.

Over a period of 10 years, I traveled to the most far-distant countries in the world annually to celebrate Thanksgiving Day and to eat the most nontraditional Thanksgiving dinners I could find. Over time, this custom took me to, among others, Hobart, Tasmania, the stomping ground of swashbuckler Errol Flynn; Katmandu, Nepal, the Himalayan home of the Abominable Snowman; and Nairobi, Kenya, the last outpost of civilization in the heart of safari country. I even sailed up the Ganges and down the Amazon to add more twists to my annual celebration.

At each stop, I tried to choose a dining spot that reflected the history and culture of the country I was visiting. I also attempted to select (and to eat, if humanly possible) the kind of indigenous cuisine that modern pilgrims would most likely serve for their Thanksgiving Day feast.

Sometimes the gastronomic rewards of my Thanksgiving Day forays were worth the effort, not to mention the considerable airfare. Other times the whole experience left me longing for all the traditional fixings. And, of course, it wasn't always easy trying to order Thanksgiving dinner in countries where people didn't know what Thanksgiving is all about.

The first year I celebrated Thanksgiving on Bali, one of the most enchanting islands in Indonesia. Even now I can still picture the blazing red sunsets over Kuta Beach and smell the heavy perfume of the tropical flowers. On Thanksgiving Day, I found a small open-air restaurant with a canopy of palm leaves that seemed perfect for the occasion. When I asked the Balinese waiter if he had turkey on the menu, I hit a snag.

In response to his look of bewilderment, I tried to explain that a turkey was something like a big chicken, and I demonstrated by flapping my arms and gobbling. Everyone else in the restaurant paused for a few seconds, their forks frozen in midair. For a minute, there was a flicker of recognition in the waiter's eyes. He soon returned carrying a very large platter.

As it turned out, he was close. But, as they say, no cigar. It was a platter of grilled turtle rather than grilled turkey, the former a delicacy of the Balinese.

A new-found friend from New Zealand, who was also vacationing there and had offered to celebrate Thanksgiving with me, said she thought the turtle tasted a bit like grilled goat, kind of chewy and well spiced. I didn't argue the point since I'd never sampled grilled goat, either. At least the meal was edible.

There have been times, however, when it wasn't.

One Thanksgiving, I booked a jungle cruise down a 350-mile stretch of the Amazon River from Iquitos, Peru, to Tabatinga, Brazil. The minute I stepped aboard the Rio Amazonas, a converted banana hauler that was to be our "Love Boat" for four days, I buttonholed the cook and requested he prepare something special, something very Amazonian for my Thanksgiving dinner. I specifically asked for piranha, thinking what an ironic twist it would be to end up eating man-eating fish for Thanksgiving instead of the other way around. But luck was against me. One of the crewmembers told me when I sat down at the table on Thanksgiving Day that we would not be entering piranha waters until the next morning. That meant my plate of pan-fried piranha would end up becoming a belated Thanksgiving dinner.

But the crew did not disappoint me that Thanksgiving night. They brought out a covered dish and set it in front of me with great fanfare. Off came the lid, revealing half of a grilled anteater that had been captured by a local Indian tribe, former headhunters as I later found out.

More precisely, it was half of a very old anteater that had been burned to a crisp. It was shoe-leather tough and I found I couldn't cut it, chop it, tear it apart, bite it or chew it. Even dousing it with the locally made hot sauce, which was guaranteed to burn a hole in your stomach lining, didn't help. Fortunately, the meal included other Amazonian trimmings such as potatoes, rice and bananas, so I didn't go hungry.

Selecting just the right restaurant, one that reflected the history and culture of the country and served indigenous foods, was an important factor in my Thanksgiving Day quest. One year I headed Down Under and made my way to Tasmania, a strange apple-shaped island off the southeastern shore of Australia. Tasmania was originally settled as a penal colony, and among the top tourist attractions today are the Colonial Convict Museum and the ruins of the Port Arthur prison complex. In view of the island's dubious history, I thought the logical choice of dining spots would be the Ball and Chain Restaurant in Hobart, the birthplace of actor Errol Flynn.

I wasn't disappointed. The dank-as-a-dungeon dining room was done up in 19th-century penal colony decór, complete with iron bars, rough-hewn wooden tables and even a pillory for customers who didn't pay their bills. The waiters and waitresses were dressed in period prison garb, and the background music was a motley collection of Australian beer drinking songs. I passed up the "penitentiary chicken" and the "condemned man's reprieve" and decided to go with a gigantic Tasmanian crayfish served up Mornay style with a cheese and wine sauce. It more than lived up to its billing that night.

Although I had originally planned to celebrate Thanksgiving the next year in Monrovia, the capital of Liberia (for some reason, the idea struck my fancy even though Liberia's only real claim to culinary fame is baked barracuda), the timing turned out wrong. Instead, I ended up in Nairobi, Kenya, on November 24, searching for some restaurant that served native African food. There were virtually none except the African Heritage Cafe on Kenyatta Avenue. I later learned why when I persuaded the chef, a tiny lady with thick glasses named Mamatin, to prepare a sampling of indigenous dishes especially for me.

To be perfectly honest, there is only so much you can do with corn, beans and potatoes. Even under the most skillful direction, it will never qualify as haute cuisine. In the end, the names of the dishes—"viesi," "boga," "gatheru," "irio" and "skuma wiki"—turned out to be much more interesting than the ingredients.

At times, the place rather than the meal itself was the real attraction for Thanksgiving.

One year while, visiting Easter Island, which is famous for its monolithic carved statues but not for its restaurants, I enjoyed a Thanksgiving picnic under the palms at Anakena Beach with my tour companions. It was at that same idyllic spot back in 450 A.D. that Hotu Matua, the island's first self-proclaimed king, landed with his seafaring settlers. Centuries later in 1955, Norwegian explorer Thor Heyerdahl set up his rustic camp on Anakena Beach and began his extensive excavation of the island.

Our Thanksgiving meal that day included much of the same fare—chicken, bread, fruit and juice—that both Hotu Matua and Heyerdahl could very well have eaten when they were on Anakena Beach themselves.

Have I ever broken my Thanksgiving tradition by eating American food? No, but I have been tempted.

In Jerusalem I came very close to hunkering down with a big juicy burger, French fries and a shake at a McDavid's fast-food restaurant. Fortunately, my better sense prevailed and I decided to go to the Hahoma, the only kosher restaurant in the old Jewish Quarter of the city back in 1984.

In this case, selecting the main course was simple: St. Peter's fish, which is found only in the Sea of Galilee, was the perfect choice. There is a legend behind this particular fish, I discovered. In Biblical times, the Romans heavily taxed the people of Capernaum, and on one occasion when there was no money, St. Peter directed the villagers to lower their nets into the sea.

The fish they caught turned out to have a gold coin in its mouth, which saved them from the ravages of the Roman tax collectors. This legend also explains why St. Peter's fish is always served with its head on.

As luck would have it, my fish was short on gold coins that

night, so I had to ante up the shekels to pay for my Thanksgiving dinner all by myself.

Finding a suitable restaurant in Old Malacca, a weathered seaport on the western coast of Malaysia, proved to be much more difficult. After having been ruled successively by the Chinese, Portuguese, Dutch and British, the city should have been able to offer at least a modicum of good Occidental and Oriental cuisine. Guess again.

The driver of my trishaw (a three-wheel bike with a passenger seat in front) was panting by the time he finally dropped me off in front of the Lim Tian Puan, a Chinese restaurant, one rainy Thanksgiving night. We had been circling past small, dirty-looking street cafes for nearly an hour and I figured the Lim Tian Puan was probably my last prospect for a decent meal. I was ushered into the dining room by a Chinese woman and seated at a small table draped in a red cloth. No one around me, including my waitress, spoke anything but Chinese. However, the menu items had English translations, so I was able to make my choices without wild guesswork.

I passed up the shark's fin with scrambled eggs in favor of spiced teochew duck, the restaurant's specialty, bean curd with crabmeat and fried rice. After a moment's hesitation, I added steamed-pig's-brain-with-chicken-leg soup to my order. In Asia, just about any plant or animal part is considered fair game for the dinner table, and I was curious to see how the cook would handle that combination.

Half an hour later, my food arrived. The waitress smiled as she ladled my gray soup broth with whole chicken feet floating in it out of the pot into my bowl. I decided to start with something more palatable looking and took a spoonful of the bean curd with crabmeat. It looked, and tasted, a little like tiny pillows of soggy foam rubber.

The spiced teochew duck was excellent and reminded me of the pressed duck I had enjoyed in Chinese restaurants back home. The fried rice, flavored with bits of egg and scallion, was also worth a second forkful.

But the soup stopped me cold. I asked the Chinese woman who had seated me how I was supposed to eat it. She gestured for me to nibble the skin off the chicken feet but not to eat the bones.

I fished out a chicken foot and pulled off a piece of tough yellow skin with my teeth. That first bite convinced me I didn't want a second.

When the waitress wasn't looking, I deftly tossed all the chicken feet from my bowl back into the pot on the table and continued spooning up my soup broth, hoping I wouldn't encounter any recognizable pieces of pig's brain.

A few minutes later, the waitress came by, spotted my bowl sans chicken feet and dutifully scooped a few more out of the pot into the bowl. As soon as she wasn't looking, I threw them back into the pot.

By the time the meal was over, the chicken feet had made at least 10 jet-propelled trips back and forth, leaving the waitress somewhat mystified about the remarkable qualities of my soup pot and its bountiful contents.

It was one Thanksgiving, probably the first and hopefully the last, where I didn't bother to ask for a doggie bag.

Hold the Salad

JULIA NIEBUHR EULENBERG

WE WERE IN LONDON, at the end of my first trip to England. Even though my husband had been here before, he had left much of the planning of this trip up to me. I had depended heavily on our local bookstore, and ultimately we had followed author Rick Steves's advice. He had eased our entry into England with the warning that we should leave Heathrow and travel west immediately, never even thinking about going into London first.

Try Bath, he suggested. It's good for the soul, perfect for recovering from jet lag and not a bad place to be in any case. So, at Heathrow, we found our luggage, picked up our rail passes and caught a bus to Reading. From there, we took the train to Bath. The city was perfect. We had a lovely hotel, and we trained for all the walking that would take place over the next three weeks by exploring many inches of Bath.

We hadn't followed Steves every step of the way but had decided to end the trip with another of his recommendations.

Back in London, we would take lunch at the "palatial Criterion Restaurant . . . a world away from the punk junk of Piccadilly Circus." Though I can no longer prove it, I also seemed to remember his having said that, though expensive, the restaurant was worth the cost and that even he sometimes splurged by eating a meal there.

The Criterion is one of several restaurants designed by a young Yorkshire native who, in his early days, wouldn't have been allowed in the homes of any of the rich and elegant who chose to dine in his establishments. We walked into a dimmed room, so dim in fact that I had to check twice to be sure I'd taken off my sunglasses. I had. We were probably already in trouble. My husband prefers to dine where he can see the food. As a result, we do not have a dimmer switch in our dining room.

Two young women clad in black elegance greeted us at the desk. "Two?" one of them asked, eyeing our less than elegant tourist clothing and bags.

"Yes," we concurred. "And might you have a nonsmoking section?"

"No," they murmured, "But if someone is smoking next to your table, we can move you."

With that, we were led past an occasional table of diners. These were women dressed in elegant suits and little black dresses and a few men in suits. We were seated at a table near the back of the restaurant, directly across from the kitchen doors. Few would need to pass our table and be astonished at our choice of luncheon clothing, unless they needed to go to the restroom.

The waiter suggested several options, all verging on a full meal, which neither of us really wanted. I ordered a Caesar salad, "without the bacon, please," I said firmly, looking up at the waiter. A few days earlier I had made the same request to a steward on the train, and he had recommended against it. "Without

the bacon, it's pointless. There's only a few bits of lettuce other-
wise." I forebore telling him—or the waiter at the Criterion—
that no self-respecting "traditional" Caesar salad—which both
menus proclaimed—would dream of containing bacon. In any
case, the Criterion's waiter had no problem with my request,
perhaps because there were also anchovies on the salad, thus
eliminating the problem of only a few bits of lettuce.

By the time our order had been taken, a young lad had arrived with our silverware and glasses. He then went on to set
several empty tables around us. The sounds of clinking glassware and silver suddenly made the restaurant sound fuller, as
if a new luncheon crowd had just been seated, even though
we were as few as ever.

As soon as we had placed our meal order and requested
a bottle of sparkling water, the lad was back to remove the
wine glasses. Meanwhile, a maiden was proffering bread
from a large basket.

"Yes," I said. "I'd like a piece." But when I inquired about
a bread plate, I was told there weren't bread plates and I
should just put it on the tablecloth. Right! Wine glass, water
glass, two forks, two knives, hovering waiters and other min-
ions—and the bread goes on the table.

My husband ordered two starters, rather than a full meal—
risotto with saffron and a Salade Niçoise. I ordered only the
Caesar salad. I finished my salad and he his risotto, and then we
waited for the large staff to clear these dishes away and bring his
salad. During the long interim, we had a great deal to watch.

Tables were cleared, breadcrumbs were scraped with small
metal scrapers into waiters' hands, bread was proffered and
glasses were moved, added and removed. Silver was rear-
ranged and patted in place. Napkins were folded and placed
just so. Sometimes this action took place at our own table;

sometimes the rearranging was done at nearby tables. It was, in short, a perfectly choreographed dance better suited to the Mad Hatter's Tea Party than to an efficiently run restaurant.

The ceiling was quite lovely, a point Steves had made. It was composed of mosaics of unknown design and some gilt ones, so that the whole effect was one of sparkling highlights in a seeming effort to defeat the low-wattage lamps directed upward at them.

A young man whisked away our clean plates. Another poured one glass and then another from our water bottle, until finally it was empty. Someone else arrived to remove it. The breadbasket girl attempted to remove my bread, which I had carelessly placed on the butter plate, unwilling to put it on the table, despite her gentle recommendation.

Still no salad. My husband was beginning to wonder what was happening, and we were starting to snicker. All this meaningless activity and no one was really serving us! And then, for a moment, we got our hopes up. A young man came up to our table, but it was no good, it couldn't be the salad because he was wearing the wrong color of coat. He's dressed only in white; the waiters had all worn black. Indeed, he had come merely to scrape unwanted breadcrumbs from our table.

I resisted looking at my husband until the white-coated minion had left, then commented, "I knew it; I knew that was next!"

In the midst of all this elegance and fine food, two mild odors hovered, like the waiters. Cigarette smoke wafted gently toward us from two tables away—a cigarette held discreetly so it would annoy no one at its own table, but aimed toward the rest of us. The other odor made us wonder even more about the state of mind of the management. I asked the way to the restroom. A young lady pointed the way and said, "I'm afraid you'll have to use the Gents', they're painting the Women's."

Left unsaid, but possibly revealed in the surprise on my face, was the thought "In the middle of the day? When the restaurant is open and serving meals?"

All I said was that I wouldn't mind if I didn't have to share. But when I passed the door and saw a man entering, it was quite clear that I might have to. So I simply kept walking until I reached the ladies' room. Two men stood in front of it, one wearing a white waiter's coat, the other a polo shirt.

"Hello, madam, mind the paint. It's wet. Only the black paint, madam!"

I "minded" the paint and managed not to get any on myself. Meantime, the painters had moved on to the Gents'. One can only hope that this was quick-drying paint since the dinner hour was fast approaching and a more elegantly and expensively dressed clientele might not want to be expected to "mind the paint." All this meant that eventually my husband had to use the ladies' room.

He returned to the table and commented, "This place is getting on my nerves."

Are you still waiting in suspense for him to receive his salad? I have kept nothing from you. We were still waiting too.

Suddenly a black-coated waiter appeared at our table, as the gentle moving of silver and glassware at empty tables continued in the background. "Would you like anything more?" he inquired.

In civilized tones, my husband said, "I'd like what I ordered, the Salade Niçoise."

The waiter reeled slightly, then recovered, apologized and with quick hand movements set the others in motion again. Out of nowhere appeared silverware. Someone asked, "Would you like more water, something else to drink, perhaps?"

The large green bottle of mineral water had long since been emptied and removed. "No, we wouldn't," we replied.

A butter plate reappeared, and then the basket girl bearing bread. My husband took one, I declined.

As yet another waiter hovered, my husband requested a dessert menu and said, "She will be having dessert, and we'll want it served with my salad so she won't have to wait, watch me eat and then be served."

"Oh, yes, sir, sorry, sir." The black-coated waiter came over, reassured my husband it would be just a moment for the salad— "terribly sorry, sir"—and took my order for a lemon tart.

Truth to tell, the tart, like the rest of the food, was very good. Creamy and lemony, the way a true lemon pie should be. Real anchovies, fresh, white flesh, skin still on them and delicately flavored, not tinned or brined, had topped the Caesar salad, along with delicate slices of fine Parmesan cheese. A real piece of freshly cooked tuna sat atop the Salade Nicoise. Strands of real saffron had been arrayed on top of the risotto. The silver was heavy, yet comfortable to use. The salt and pepper shakers stood on four little feet. The napkins and cloths were white and nicely starched.

In other words, the cooking was first class, and the milieu was that of a fine restaurant. I'm sure the service was intended to fit this mode as well. The problem was that it was so overdone as to be preposterous, pompous and annoying. Maintaining our own good American manners, we waited until we were outside in the more raucous space of Piccadilly Circus to look at each other and snort derisively. It was certainly, since we were in a good frame of mind and not starving, worth the experience. But it was most definitely not the experience we had expected.

How I Became a Purveyor of Caviar and Champagne on the Trans-Siberian

Alev Lytle Croutier

In the late sixties, Trans-Siberian had not yet become a sybaritic tourist extravaganza but served as a humble transportation vehicle that the Soviets graciously allowed other world citizens, who weren't fussy about their accommodations, to experience.

Carrying an English translation of Chairman Mao's "little red book," *The Thoughts of Chairman Mao,* which still was Chinese to me, I started my journey from Tokyo, my domicile for the past year, to the Cannes film festival, for the screening of a film I had worked on.

I imagined two weeks of gliding through expansive snow-covered plateaus, encountering larger-than-life figures resembling Omar Sharif and Geraldine Chaplin riding troikas in great furs, barbed-wired fences around torture camps from which no one returned, and a glimpse of the old Silk Road on which my ancestors had slowly trekked their way westward. I imagined myself disguised as a foreign correspondent or a

71

great woman spy who would stumble upon some dark secret and become a pawn in a chain of impossible intrigues. After all, I was young and entitled to such fantasies.

My story begins at the port of Nakhodka, at the exchange counter. Utterly inept in dealing with money calculation, I had developed the habit of converting all my cash into the currency of the country I was entering—in this case around five hundred dollars' worth of yen into rubles. And when I say all, I mean all.

We boarded the train in Khabarovsk and traveled through Siberia, vast stretches of verdant lands, mountains and plains, interspersed with colorless towns of lonely people who came everyday to wave at the train. Occasionally, we stopped to eat in those towns, a welcome opportunity since the train food tasted like dishwater. Our two "in-tourist" guides (synonym for KGB), named Andrei and Natasha, accompanied us everywhere.

Just as we were arriving at the last station before exiting the USSR, a voice came over the intercom. You must get rid of all your rubles before crossing the border. It is forbidden to take any Soviet currency abroad, Natasha translated.

At the exchange counter, I flashed my rubles and the record of the initial exchange at Nakhodka. The guy behind the counter shook his head and said, "Nyett."

"Nyett what? No yen. I don't care. In fact I'd prefer French francs."

"We can only give you back the currency you exchanged from and we do not have any yen here," he repeated.

"It's all right," I said. "I'll take anything, francs, dollars, pounds."

"We can only give you back the original currency."

"Then what am I supposed to do?"

He shrugged. "Either return them to us or you must spend it all here."

I inquired about returning to Moscow but my visa expired that very day and I had no choice but to leave the USSR immediately. I could not sneak out my rubles since I had already exposed them to the authorities; besides they would do me no good abroad, having zero value on the world money market.

The prospect of arriving penniless in Paris was devastating. Where would I stay? What would I eat? I contemplated the railroad tracks, remembering Anna Karenina. My train comrades were sympathetic but helpless as I gazed at their consolatory faces.

Since I'd rather die than allow this border town bureaucracy the satisfaction of confiscating my last pennies without a decent return, I marched into the little gift shop full of the usual mementos one finds in border towns all over the world, even the communist world: lacquered boxes, fake icons, babushka dolls. (How many babushka dolls would I get for five hundred dollars?) Caspian caviar, Champagne and vodka. That was it. I'd venture into my doom, plastered and debauched.

Suddenly, I had become a heroine in this tiny municipality. Crates of caviar, vodka, and Champagne were delivered to my compartment by a retinue of happy sales clerks and porters.

Back on the train, I popped the cork and toasted my way into oblivion as we crossed the agricultural fields of the Ukraine into Poland. Soon, a few of my fellow passengers joined to partake in my fatalistic endeavor. Others, looking for diversion, popped in, and offered to buy some of my Champagne and caviar. Why not? I'd need a metro ticket in Paris. Drop the money in my tote bag.

As the days advanced, the motley stack of world currency grew, the spirits and the fish eggs diminished rapidly, and, under the influence, a great deal of intimacies were shared. Everyone on the train had become bosom buddies as the conductor announced, "Gare de Lyon." I splashed some water on my face to wake up and quickly gathered my belongings.

I handed the stash from my tote bag to the guy at the exchange—dollars, marks, pounds, liras. Obviously annoyed, he swore at me in French first, then handed me around seven hundred dollars worth of francs. I thought he'd miscalculated. Not only had I retrieved my original amount but I showed a good profit. The pleasures of free enterprise.

I jumped into a cab and smiled all the way to my Left Bank hotel, amazed at the scheme of things. The "red book" was abandoned in the backseat for the next passenger.

The Last Supper

Mark Cerulli

I couldn't read the menu, but the dish was right there in the Tokyo restaurant's window—translucent slices of white flesh, gossamer thin, artfully arranged in an overlapping circular pattern. Each tender piece looked like the petal of a flower. It was the mythical morsel—fugu.

Almost unavailable in America, fugu is the Mount Everest of sushi, a dish that, if not exactingly prepared, will kill you. That's why the chefs who serve it up have to be specially licensed by Japan's health ministry and trained for up to ten years.

Despite the exotic name, fugu is actually common blowfish. You might have seen one stuffed and inflated in a tourist shop, or finning around off the Florida coast or Jersey shore. As anybody who watches the Discovery Channel knows, Nature is a bitch, so this meek-looking fish found two ways to stay alive: inflating its body with air to appear larger than it is (not fatal) and secreting a highly toxic tetrodotoxin from no less than 11 different body parts—including the skeleton (definitely fatal). The toxin itself causes total muscle paralysis while leaving the brain completely intact. In other words, you can't move an eyelid, but your brain is screaming "HELP MEEEE!" Eventually you die from lack of oxygen. (Although they say if you are hustled onto a ventilator, you can last until the toxins pass through your system.)

It all comes down to the cutting—how skilled the chef is in removing the dangerous organs. Still, even with all the training, precautions and warnings, a handful of diners die each year in Japan from improperly prepared fugu. Imagine . . . the chef gets a phone call . . . is worried about paying his Amex bill or yesterday's fight with the wife and Shazam—his blade nicks the liver and game over. (To be fair, the art of preparing fugu is just that—an art, handed down over centuries. The chefs and the Japanese government take it very seriously.) Even fugu leftovers—the parts the chef can't use—are treated like spent nuclear fuel rods. Restaurants seal them in special containers for shipment to a fugu waste site where they are disposed of in a chemical bath. (The fugu toxin is immune to heat.) This after several Japanese homeless people died from eating raw fugu bodyparts fished out of restaurant dumpsters.

Still, deadly or not, trying fugu had always been in the back of my mind. It was one of those conveniently next-to-impossible activities like running with the bulls or going shark cage diving in Great White territory. Yeah, you could do it, but would you?

My wife and I had arrived in Tokyo the night before—it was her business trip and I had just glommed on. We stayed at the grand old Okura hotel and I arranged to meet a friend named Makoto, a salaryman who lived in one of the city's suburbs. "Let's have dinner," I said, ". . . and hey, know anyplace that serves fugu?" In the West, when you make a request, people are liable to just blow it off, or "forget." In Japan, they are *on* it, especially if you are a guest. Fugu I wanted, fugu I'd get! That's how I found myself outside a chain restaurant called Sagami near Tokyo's shopping mecca, the Ginza.

As we walked in, my inner mind gremlin started. "You're not really going to eat that, are you?" it asked. A hostess sat us, we ordered a round of sake and the menus came out. "Relax," I told myself, "there's plenty of time to bail on this . . ." Inside the laminated menu, there it was again, a photograph of the deadly dish, framed by text I couldn't even begin to read. We ordered some appetizers and sushi and sure enough, Makoto pointed to the fugu and said something in rapid fire Japanese. The waiter jotted it all down and left. The deed was done. The rest of the meal I don't remember. What I do remember is the waiter setting down an elegant dark plate with the fugu-sashi arranged in several elaborate circles. (I later found out it was meant to resemble a chrysanthemum, the Japanese flower of death.)

Makoto speared a slice, so I grabbed for one with my chopsticks and . . . nothing. I found the taste to be kind of rubbery, maybe even downright bland. But still, this was fugu and I had to eat more. Even my wife, bless her, ate a couple of slivers. "If anything's happening to you, it's happening to me." she said.

A few slices later I began to feel something—not the faint tingling of the palate a master fugu chef creates by leaving just the barest trace of toxin—instead I was feeling hot, uncomfortably so. Well, it was winter and I had a sweatshirt on, so I doffed that. But then I began feeling dizzy. Suddenly the crowded restaurant seemed a bit too bright. "Say, uh, you've had fugu here before, right?" I tossed out as casually as I could. Makoto, busily eating, said no. He rarely eats fugu, but when he does, "Usually I go to a place that specializes in fugu." Okay . . . I won't say I felt faint, but I wasn't feeling too chipper either. "Toldja" the mind gremlin said, already dancing on my coffin. I gulped down my water. Makoto ate more fugu. At other tables, people talked, laughed and puffed away. The wait staff circulated with plates of raw fish, steaming bowls of exotic soup, and mugs of cold beer. Finally Makoto put down his chopsticks. He had had enough and so had I. Check please! (The price was actually quite reasonable—somewhere around $60 a person.)

Out on the street as we moved through the crowds I began to feel better, the cold air actually felt good on my clammy skin. Maybe it was too hot, or I was too tired. My wife and I took a costly cab ride back to our hotel—where even in my addled state I noticed the door opened and closed by remote control and the cab driver wore lacy white gloves.

The next morning I woke up, experimentally wiggled my toes and took a few deep breaths. I felt fine, and so did my wife. Outside, the sun was shining, the traffic was moving, the uniformed construction crew across the street was doing calisthenics in a happy group. There was no sloppy chef; my momentary health blip was just the souvenir of our 6,000-mile trip—plain old jet lag.

THE THOUSAND-YEAR-OLD FISH

PATTI DEVENEY

MY HUSBAND AND I TRAVELED throughout Europe, the Middle East and North Africa for a year and a half. We stayed at unique (nice word for cheap) hotels and hostels and ate food purchased from street vendors that should have killed us. While living in Israel, we spent five months volunteering at Kibbutz Hulda, outside Jerusalem.

On our fifth wedding anniversary, we decided to take a day trip to Galilee to celebrate. At a lovely restaurant on the Red Sea I ordered their locally caught specialty, "The Thousand-Year-Old Fish." The meal was so expensive that for the first and last time on our trip, we put it on our credit card. Later that night in Bethlehem, I started to feel very sick and dizzy. I kept stopping to sit down on the curbs, not caring that they were filthy and covered with donkey dung. Soon my husband realized something was terribly wrong. Since it was Shabbat there was no local transportation back to Jerusalem or our kibbutz. He and I walked around until we found a convent in

Bethlehem where the nuns let me in to rest. I was placed alone in a huge dorm room where there must have been 100 single cots neatly made up. That was the longest night of my life!

I must have gotten up 20 times that night to find the bathroom. I was so disoriented that each time I returned I kept crawling back into different beds. I was still sleeping the next afternoon when a kindly nun came to see if I was still alive. She reported that my dear husband had been standing downstairs for hours waiting for me to come out. We caught a bus back to the kibbutz that afternoon where I immediately sought medical advice. I was diagnosed with severe dysentery and ended up in quarantine for two weeks. There was no way they were going to let me back on kitchen duty.

The only good thing around that memorable anniversary dinner is that our MasterCard bill never made it home. The meal was free.

THE COCKROACH FLOOR SHOW

BETH ESFANDIERI

VISITING AUSTRALIA IN 1999, my husband (at the time) and I stopped off at Surfers Paradise to collect a souvenir from the Hard Rock Café. It was late and we were just in from a week on the great barrier reef. Both of us were sandy, sunburned and very hungry. On the way out of town, in a very posh neighborhood, we spied a Thai restaurant with lots of vehicles still in the lot. Inside we were almost refused service thanks to our casual attire and finally, begrudgingly, were seated in a corner near the kitchen.

The food smelled and looked divine as waiters carried heaping plates from the kitchen to other tables, and we were both more than ready to order when the waiter finally arrived. That was when a three-inch cockroach crawled out from under our tablecloth. The waiter calmly explained that this was to be expected at this time of year. Nothing to worry about. After all this was the kind of place where the cockroaches held hands to keep the walls from tumbling down.

Before the appetizers arrived, an even larger cockroach appeared on the wall next to our table; then two more crawled out of a vase holding a flower arrangement. I stood up so fast my chair tipped over, startling other diners. Suddenly, the cockroaches were doing a floor show. The wait staff began crushing them on the floor, wall and tables. The restaurant cleared out quickly and after the staff finished smashing the small invaders the employees were sent home early. Most of the diners switched to fast food joints. We never did get another chance to try this popular establishment.

I Think It Was Something I Ate

Karin Palmquist

I was sitting in a doctor's office in a small town in northern Sweden right before Christmas. It was mid-afternoon, and the sun was already setting.

A young doctor with wire rim glasses and a narrow neck entered the room and looked at my chart.

"Your birthday is coming up. So is mine. You're two years older than me."

Nice introduction. I felt old. Since when were kids younger than me allowed to be doctors?

"So how are you feeling?"

"I have a terrible stomach cramp, and I have not kept any food down for a month."

"What do you do?"

"I'm a writer. I travel a lot."

"So you think it could have been something you ate?"

I had seen the inside of doctor's offices on five continents. It was the downside of traveling. I always got sick. I came home from one trip to Central Asia a rattling 115 pounds, and that's not attractive when you're 6 feet tall, no matter what the fashion mags tells you.

"How is your stress level at work?"

Come on. Enough with the small talk. It wasn't stress. It was something I ate. It started on my trip to Egypt. Just give me something that will knock me out for a couple of days and then I'll be fine.

"These pills they gave you, in . . ." the doctor looked at the chart, "in America. They're strong enough to knock out a horse. I'd never prescribe those pills to a woman." He wrinkled his forehead for emphasis.

"But they worked," I grumbled.

"I really think we need to get to the bottom of this."

Oh no, he was one of those thorough, enthusiastic ones. Get me a jaded one who has been on his shift since Friday and would be just so happy to write me a prescription and get me out of here.

"I'd like to take a look at your intestines."

"You mean like an X-ray?"

"Not quite. It's a procedure called endoscopy. We enter the large intestine with a tiny camera."

A butt cam? Not a pretty picture.

Could this be the end of my travels?

"You have to try to be a bit more careful," the doctor sighed as he wrote out a prescription for something strong, sure to knock me out for a couple of days. It was better than an endoscopy, which I refused.

I hate being careful. Some of my best travel memories are dinner, not to mention breakfast and lunch.

In fact, one of my earliest travel memories also happens to be a meal. I was five years old, and my parents and I were driving down from our home in northern Sweden to Warsaw to visit my Polish aunt and uncle.

We disembarked from the overnight ferry in Gdansk early in the morning, before the banks opened. This was the late '70s and Poland was firmly wedged into the Eastern Bloc. The zloty was not a convertible currency. You could only get zlotys in certain Polish locations. There were no Thomas Cook desks when you stepped off the ferry, no exchange offices open 24 hours.

Instead of waiting around, we started driving toward Warsaw. All we had to eat were candy bars. The road wound down the Polish countryside, past grazing cattle and wheat fields. An old woman was walking along the side of the road, carrying a big basket. My dad pulled over and asked the woman what was in her basket.

Apples.

He tried to buy a few with Swedish money that had no value in Poland.

She peeked into the car and her face lit up at the sight of ballpoint pens.

After my father handed her the pens she said, "Papyrus, papyrus."

"Paper," my dad said, "she wants paper." My parents started scrambling around purses and bags looking for paper.

"Here," I said, holding out my coloring book.

My dad quickly bartered the coloring book for apples.

Other memories from that trip have faded, but I do remember sitting in the back seat of our old Citroen, eating my apple, wondering if the woman was coloring the book. It looked like a regular apple but tasted very different. It was a foreign apple in a foreign land. Plus my mom had cleaned it with a perfumed wet wipe.

As I grew up, the less appetizing the food experience, the more cherished the memory. I'd come home telling friends about sheep eyeballs in Kyrgyzstan and deep-fried dragonflies in Indonesia.

At a reception in Iceland my friend Marianne and I were served some huge lumps of sour-smelling meat. These were definitely not Swedish meatballs. Before refrigerators and takeout, people had to think of other creative ways to preserve food. One was pickling meat, fish and vegetables, leaving a faint smell of vinegar lingering over the island. Fair enough. We didn't mind the pickling but insisted on full disclosure.

"Ram testicles."

Really? So big? Our eyes couldn't help wandering over to the buffet table to perhaps catch a glance of the rest of the smorgasbord.

"Do you have a brother?" Marianne cooed to the ball on her plate as I tried my best to dissect mine without shooting it across the table.

Once after a visit to a mine near Karakol, Kyrgyzstan, my travel mate and I were invited to stay with a local family in a mountain village. We arrived at their house and found the whole family, plus half the village, seated around a table absolutely piled with food. A huge silver samovar filled with tea towered above the cabbage salads, tiny deep-fried, moon-shaped breads and homemade preserves. Someone had told the village people that we were vegetarians. The rumor was false, but after a certain amout of time in Kyrgyzstan and a certain amount of mystery meat, nearly every visitor becomes a vegetarian.

We sat down on one of the thick mattresses next to the table. There was no electricity, and the only source of light in the room was a kerosene lamp. Prodded by the woman of the house, we grazed on Kyrgystan haute cuisine. No one else touched the food. They were watching us chow down, waiting for us to call for seconds.

After dinner we retired to the front room of the three-room house. Seated on mattresses around a low coffee table our hostess offered us an after-dinner drink made from flour and milk. It was the middle of winter and we were at 12,000 feet. Plastic film covered the windows. Clearly these people were heeding the U.S. Department of Homeland Security advice on how to prepare for terrorists. The drink warmed our stomachs, and we emptied our glasses. The woman happily poured another round. We sat there all night, drinking with the village people. After the guests left, our hostess poured what was left of the drinks back into the bucket.

I love the way people help you appreciate their culinary culture. Of course, sometimes the joke is at your expense. You politely sample the fried caterpillars and then turn around to watch the locals snub the stuff. They don't like it. They just want to haze you like a fraternity initiate. I learned about this first-hand when, as a punishment for my sins, I became a high school exchange student in a tiny West Virginia town. I came expecting cheeseburgers and ended up sampling squirrel stew. I know the main reason they served it was to laugh at a foreigner. After all, we were there for their amusement. I learned a lot during my year in West Virginia. It was exciting to discover that you could make salad out of Jell-O and marshmallows.

Of course there are ways to play it safe. On my last visit to Kyrgyzstan, the French army brought in bottled Evian water from France for wimpy soldiers stationed just outside the Kyrgyz capital. But I can't live that way. I can't give up eating local cuisine. I'll continue eating from street kitchens even if I know that there isn't a single squirrel in the entire neighborhood.

The Best Restaurant in Town?

Marcia Muller and Bill Pronzini

WARNING: DON'T BELIEVE EVERYTHING YOU READ in travel guides. Some recommendations may be hazardous to your health.

The guide we consulted a few years ago, when we spent a night in a medium-sized Idaho city while on a driving trip, should have carried the above disclaimer. Unfortunately for us, we believed the three-star rating given to a restaurant not far from our motel. No other received more than two stars; therefore, we reasoned, this one must be the best restaurant in town.

Its physical appearance and clientele gave us no hint of its true nature. The place was attractive enough, if undistinguished, and full of normal-looking people eating what appeared from a distance to be normal-looking food. A friendly waitress showed us to a booth in an alcove near the salad bar, the last available seating. And the menus she handed us seemed to advertise an array of traditional but palatable items.

We considered. One of us decided on the lamb chops, the other opted for Southern Fried Chicken; house burgundy with the former, house white with the latter. Did we want the salad bar, the waitress asked? A leisure-suited man at a nearby table had been loudly praising the bar's selections to his companion, so we said yes.

The selections did look fairly interesting—until another man, who'd gone up ahead of us, chose to sneeze without covering his mouth and sprayed the iceberg lettuce. This wasn't the fault of the restaurant, of course, but where was the ubiquitous plastic sneeze guard we'd seen everywhere else on our trip? One of us decided to forego the salad bar after all. The other, being a braver and more adventurous soul, gathered random samples that excluded the iceberg lettuce and anything in close proximity to it.

These samples were not eaten, however. The adventurous soul's appetite for salad vanished when the leisure-suited fellow missed his mouth with a heaping forkful of cottage cheese and pasta salad—literally opened his mouth to insert said forkful, only to mysteriously upend the fork an inch and a half short. The sight of the whitish mass avalanching down his shirtfront brought on a fierce yearning for wine.

The wine arrived. The house burgundy looked and tasted pink. Not a blush type, but that suspicious, sickly variety of "rosé" that as young adults we would buy for a dollar a half-gallon. The house white, which the waitress had assured us was very dry, was in fact very sweet and contained an odd, kerosene-like piquancy. We would soon drink them both anyway.

A basket of rolls and biscuits arrived. One of us selected a roll, only to discover that it was not a roll. It resembled bread, but it was not, nor had it ever been, bread. It had been made of a concrete-like substance that could not be broken by knife, hand, teeth, or possibly even sledgehammer.

The entrees arrived. The chicken was not Southern Fried. On the outside it was Northern Cremated; on the inside it was Prime Rib Bloody. The batter in which it had been rolled was flavored with a strange mélange of spices and something black that was not pepper. The lamb chops—ah, the lamb chops! They were thin, gray, and rested on a large lettuce leaf. Something dribbled from them that may or may not have been gravy or natural juices; it resembled, and had the consistency of, crankcase oil. As we watched in awe, this liquid not only caused the lettuce leaf to shrivel but also seemed to dissolve parts of it around the edges.

Our horror by this time had given way to a kind of maniacal mirth. Whispered comments on what lay before us produced giggles and snorts that brought wary looks from some of the other diners. We might have managed to maintain at least some public decorum if the chef had not chosen that moment to emerge from the kitchen to survey his domain. He was short and unshaven and wore a tall white hat that had been crushed on top and bent at the middle; his apron and his once-white shirt were smeared with sinister-looking stains; the cigarette that hung from a corner of his mouth trailed ashes; and the smile he wore was both self-satisfied and, so it seemed to us, quite mad.

One look at this culinary specimen and we lost it completely. One of us banged a roll against the wall, and not a flake broke off; this served to prolong our laughing fit. A nearby couple, who may or may not have been finished eating, got up and hastily departed.

We finally managed to regain a semblance of control. The waitress, who now looked as though she'd taken a job at McDonald's instead, appeared to clear our table. With brilliant understatement and no discernible irony, she said she'd noticed we hadn't seemed to enjoy our dinners. For being such good sports, perhaps we'd like to have dessert on the house. She didn't elaborate as to what she meant by "such good sports." Possibly a good sport in this establishment was anyone who neither complained to the management nor attempted to bludgeon the chef to death with one of his non-bread rolls.

How could we refuse? We accepted with as much grace as we could summon. Our dessert choices, she said, were apple cobbler or bread pudding. Which would she recommend, we asked?

"Well," she said ominously, "I wouldn't recommend the pudding."

We both ordered apple cobbler.

When two dishes of it arrived we studied the brownish contents for a time. After which the following conversation took place:

"Isn't apple cobbler supposed to have crust?"

"Yes, it is."

"I don't see any crust in my dish or yours."

"Neither do I . . . Wait a minute, what's that?"

"Where?"

"There. That tiny white thing there. Is that crust?"

"I'm not going to eat it to find out. It looks like something dead floating in a bog."

The description was apt, even if the timing wasn't. We were trying not to make cackling spectacles of ourselves again when the waitress hurriedly brought our check.

We left her a generous tip; after all, none of this had been her fault and she, too, had been a good sport. As we were leaving we passed a table occupied by half a dozen police officers in uniform. None of them looked happy; in fact, a couple appeared sullen. Outside, we vowed to scrupulously obey all traffic laws on the drive back to the motel and out of town in the morning.

If the local cops were regular patrons of "the best restaurant in town," this was no place to run afoul of the law!

Sam Wo's Insult Machine, Edsel Ford Wong

Joe Kempkes

Sex, drugs, rock & roll and fabulous food—not necessarily in that order—have been among the most popular attractions of the San Francisco Bay Area during the past half century. Some of us came here and left after one wild weekend in the 1960s; some of us are still here.

Those who arrived as part of the hedonistic wing of the baby-boomer generation were immediately in their element—no instructions were required. People who showed up with 50,000 shares of blue chip preferred, Stanford Law degrees or movie star good looks came to the right place to take advantage of their social cachet. Others were fleeing oppressive laws and narrow-minded people. For many this was the place to begin a new life or reconfigure an old one. For some lucky pilgrims, the Bay Area was Mecca, Oz and over the rainbow all rolled into one.

As in any vibrantly evolving society, we bonded through our cultural affinities. The sex, drugs and music fans headed to the bars and clubs and often lived in the Haight-Ashbury or the Castro. "Food," that other part of the cultural equation, became a defining element: what we ate and where we ate it told us something about who we were and what we were becoming.

I like to think of Sam Wo's Restaurant in San Francisco's Chinatown as perhaps the archetypal dining experience for its time and place. Everyone eventually made it there from the Montgomery Street suits who heard about it in Herb Caen's *SF Chronicle* column to the army of stoners with late-night munchies.

Occasionally a tourist happened by who hadn't been forewarned about the legendary waiter Edsel Fong Wong. In sheer terms of local color, Edsel was our 20th-century equivalent of the eccentric Emperor Norton. Norton wandered around 19th-century San Francisco in a plumed hat passing out "money" with his picture on it. Emperor Edsel was a food fight waiting to happen, a whirling tyrannical culinary experience, an opera star with Tourette syndrome. When you climbed the steep, narrow steps at Sam Wo's you did so knowing that you were about to get spanked and you had better like it. And, if you didn't leave a big tip, don't even thing about coming back. Edsel was famous for refusing to serve soft drinks, especially Coke. "No Coke!" he would shout. "Go across the street." When Edsel barked at you "Hurry up and eat, we need this table!" you didn't dare look up but reached for your fortune cookie instead. Only later, safe on the streets below would you marvel at the verbal abuse that Edsel dealt out. At parties you would trade "Edsel" stories and sometimes do impersonations, meat cleaver in hand.

Recently I dropped into Sam Wo's and was told that Edsel

was no longer there. I sat down and watched a waiter take a lunch order at an adjoining table with complete indifference to his customers. You went to Sam Wo's for the dim sum, but it was the Edsel show that made you want to return.

No longer would guests stand in line to secure one of Edsel's table. Without him a trip to Sam Wo's felt like going to your favorite steakhouse and being told you could no longer order filet mignon. His departure was a great leap backward for the city's dining scene. What an insult to San Francisco's body politic.

No Meat, No Fish—No Eat

Chris Mears

"No meat, no fish—no eat!" screamed the Italian woman at Portofino, a popular Mediterranean resort. It was a pity, as my husband, children and I were particularly hungry and a plateful of spaghetti in a rich tomato sauce with perhaps a sprinkling of tasty Italian cheese would have gone down a treat. One and two halves of our family are vegetarian, and these were the days before vegetarians were regarded as almost normal people who ate.

The Italian café proprietor lady relented and soon reappeared with large portions of spaghetti and delicious sauce, totally innocent of dead flesh.

We lived in Rhodesia (now called Zimbabwe) at the time, and we were used to odd meals, and odd reactions to our diet, which generally called up poor food when eating out. Our holiday travels often took us to game reserves like Kruger National Park in South Africa. Here the menu was alive with dead animals: buffalo steaks and roast antelope. To me, it seemed strange to spend hours driving around saying "Ah" and "How sweet" when we came across a family of impala, and then return to the camp and eat part of one.

But there is one dish prevalent in South African game reserve cafes, indeed in South Africa generally—toasted cheese and tomato sandwiches. This is the only vegetarian dish—why? A better solution is to cook your own baked potatoes on the campfires outside each hut, and even make a salad. You may have to sit inside because of the mosquitoes in the evening, and miss the glorious star-spangled spectacle of the night sky and the cries of the hyenas and wandering male lions. At breakfast you must defend your fruit from the monkeys and baboons—vital if you can't eat the biltong and outlandish frozen and bony fish from the camp shop.

Evening meals at the camp restaurant in the game park are a disaster for vegetarians. Settle for vegetables only and they arrive wet in gravy (buffalo, zebra—worse?) in spite of clear instructions to the perplexed and totally uncomprehending waiter. But there's always the sliced oranges for dessert.

In Russia the vegetarian dish that appeared every day was cabbage, wrapped in a kind of hard batter. Very strange! The same small iced tarts also appeared every meal on a plate in the middle of the table, their cherries dead center and totally untouched by tourist hand. We were cowards. Were the next batch of tourists presented with the same plateful, or did the cook create new ones, solid and forbidding, even when fresh?

Most countries appear to have their own traditional dishes for airing out on vegetarians. I remember, when young, hitch-hiking around Scotland and being given very soft-boiled eggs (ugh!) and hard, stale scones—for high tea and breakfast—by unsympathetic, elderly land-ladies in their cold Victorian boarding houses. In France, it was omelets all the way: deliciously cooked, of course. But whoever heard of people, even English people, not enamored of foie gras and small roasted birds?

Then there are dishes to send a vegetarian screaming into a corner. On Lake Malawi, in Central Africa, my non-vegetarian husband, Martin, ordered mtemba—wishing to try a local dish. Our young daughter eyed the mound of little sardinelike fishes on his plate. "Dad, you're not going to eat that, are you?" she asked. (She kept little fishes in a tank at home.) Dad didn't want anything, suddenly.

In China, Martin voluntarily picked out every piece of meat from the stewlike dinner dish. We had seen the caged dogs in the market. They were not for sale as pets.

You Say Potato, I Say Ptomaine

Roger Rapoport

When California publisher Cynthia Frank signed up for a Chicago convention her partner and husband told her she'd best book a single and go without him. "I was in Chicago in 1968," he apologized, "and they arrested me. My stomach still heaves when I think of the food they served in jail."

Thanks to her first-rate staff, there would be no problem managing the booth without him. The first night she invited editor Sal Glynn, salesman and chef/caterer Mark Wallace and publicist Teresa Simon to dinner at a Thai restaurant. After a long afternoon setting up their booth at the McCormick Place they were hot, hungry and ready to play. Dinner first, followed by a show at Buddy Guy's Legends.

Frank slept soundly that night in her Essex Inn room, not realizing that her colleagues were putting the Michigan Avenue establishment's plumbing to a serious test.

"Ptomaine is not fun," says Frank. "First you're afraid you're gonna die; then you're afraid you're not gonna die. Sal and Mark were hit so hard by the nasty bug they hallucinated as they crawled to and from the facilities." Although their needs were violent and immediate, they were able to take turns, "passing one another on hands and knees like foundering ships on a coal black night."

At dawn Frank could tell from the sounds next door that Simon wasn't doing well either. Then the publisher noticed a whimpering sound at the door. It was Wallace outside, lying on the carpet.

"I can't walk," he told her, "We'll try to meet you at the McCormick Center in a few hours if we're not dead." Without another word he turned around and crawled away.

At the convention hall, Frank finished setting up. Wallace came lurching down the aisle looking rather green.

"Thought you could use some help. Gotta chair? Omigod, where's the head?" Simon was ill, he reported, and Glynn, overcome with dehydration, had drunk his way through the in-room refrigerator and was now besieging room service.

"Would you pick up some Gatorade on your way back to the hotel?

Frank ran to a meeting and returned to the booth for an author reading. Wallace returned to his room, replaced by Glynn, who propped himself up in a corner of the booth looking like a cardboard celebrity cutout. He emitted brief sentences, punctuated by low moans.

"I'm afraid to sit down."

"Somebody stole the damn T-shirts."

"Teresa is desiccated, gesticulated, defecated."

"I'm going back to the hotel."

"Don't forget the Gatorade."

When the show closed, Frank headed across downtown looking for a grocery. She found one on a side street populated by blowing trash, winos and mangy dogs. It was a store out of her childhood. A slow fan in the ceiling stirred slower flies. A wood floor, dust on all the jars and can tops. She found a flavor of Gatorade that was no longer made and purchased three large bottles.

On her way out the clerk said: "Welcome back, honey! We haven't seen you here in a while."

At the hotel, the crew was recovering. Everyone was convinced the culprit was the peanut sauce in the blue bowl. Frank said a prayer of thanks to her special lemongrass angel who placed the red bowl closer to her hand.

Wallace, ever the caterer, suggested a visit to the Thai restaurant was in order: "We don't want anyone else to go through this, right? We'll be discreet. We'll tell them to throw out the peanut sauce and start over. If they insist, we'll have a pot of tea with the manager and theorize why the reclining Buddha is so supine."

The restaurant manager was skeptical. "Sick? You don't look sick." Glynn offered to throw up on his shoes. The manager said, "You don't fool me with this trick."

Wallace explained that they weren't trying to sue. "Sue?" the manager heard. "You dare to accuse my cook of making you rich."

When the owner showed up, Frank was amazed: "He frothed and shook like a fine Béarnaise, accused us of being worse than Cambodians and then searched for something worse, finally, with great satisfaction calling us 'book reviewers.'" Soon the group was chatting with the restaurant's attorney in a quiet corner of the restaurant. After a long conversation the attorney told the manager to give the Californians a credit on their dinner.

The manager was delighted: "We fix you dinner to die for."

THE FIRST AND LAST MEAL

CAROLE L. PECCORINI

I AM WAITING FOR MY FIRST EVENING MEAL IN BORNEO. I can see the black sky through chinks in the guesthouse roof, which explains why my mattress is slightly soggy. I learn later that the orangutans love to peel the shingles off the roof with a chomp-and-toss routine. It is 9:00 p.m. when the metal gong brrrooooongs. I slip on my flip-flops and join the other Earth-watch volunteers picking our way down the path toward the kitchen and dining enclosure. Our flashlight beams shift light from side to side, detecting puddles and gnarling roots, tangles of hanging vines, and finally a vast wave of fire ants crossing in front of us. We leap and duck, eager to reach the gentle glow of the kerosene lanterns and our dinner.

The stack of discarded shoes by the door grows. We snatch up our metal plates and a large oval spoon. As I head for a bench, I see that insects with white papery wings have also filled the room. Thousands are circling in a flight pattern, seemingly unorganized, but veering from any direct human hit.

102

"Flying termites," Professor Birute Galdikas announces, a hint of glee in her welcome. "A delicacy." I can't take my eyes off the opening and closing of her mouth. As she talks, winged termites swoop near the tide of her breath. "A cyclical event," she continues.

The jasmine rice is passed in a large metal bowl along with dark chard-like greens cooked in Indonesian spices, and small crisp fishes with eyes and fins intact.

"Pass the tea." Birute is smiling. Her eyes are warm. Three young orangutans are hanging on the screens, piqued with their own natural curiosity about human behavior. Their coppery hair stands two inches straight up on their heads and shoulders, which gives them a look of constant surprise.

Suddenly, the flying termites begin to die. First one, two, three drop and rain down on our plates, the rice and fish, our tins of hot tea. The floor and tables are littered. The Dayak men and women grab several empty bowls and begin scooping them up. Mounds of winged carcasses are ceremonially carried to the kitchen to fry. We roll our eyes.

"Do you think they are actually going to serve us fried flying termites?"

Before this thought can be fully digested, an alert goes out. "Get your feet up, quick."

A full battalion of fire ants has come up through the floorboards and is swarming across the floor to harvest the dead termites for themselves. We hold our feet in the air. I snatch up my spoon and take another serving of rice and vegetables. My thigh and lower back muscles are quivering as the parade of bowls returns from the kitchen with piping hot and crunchy insects.

This was not included in the professor's arrival lecture on the ten most likely ways you can die or get wounded in the rain forest. I had pictured dead wood falling 300 feet from the canopy and vipers that jump and leeches flipping end over end to attach themselves to my too-warm body for a blood meal. There are vibrant caterpillars that inflict intense pain, and plants that cause itching so fierce you want to tear your skin off with your own fingernails. And then the most disturbing warning of all . . .

"Orangutans rape women." When you go into the forest, we were told, wear long pants, long sleeves, and a hat. Don't speak above a whisper so the higher pitch of your voice will be disguised. Don't go out during your period. Carry a stick around camp, and always walk with another person.

We met Apollo Bob the day we arrived. Birute raised this abandoned baby orangutan at the camp and plans to return him to the rain forest as a young adult. Although orangutan youngsters would crawl into our arms to cuddle as a daily routine, she assured us that it is normal for an adolescent to have nothing but sex on his mind. Apollo Bob posted himself outside the guesthouse door.

"Don't even think about it, Apollo Bob," I warned each time he slowly turned his dark stare on me. "Don't you even think about it."

I survived three weeks without any dire calamities. I warded off leeches with Jungle Juice around the tops of my boots and along my shoelaces. I fell into a fetid swamp and bathed in the black water river. We witnessed the capture of a dragon-fish poacher who was put in charge of the evidence of his own crime according to Indonesian custom. And my yellow mesh T-shirt is now tie-dyed from being washed in buckets that did not include sorting dark from light.

Last meals are important rituals in Indonesia. There are speeches to make, gifts to wrap, foods to prepare. At last the gong clangs. At 10:00 p.m. we head out on a final trek down the trail of roots, puddles, and ants. My flashlight batteries are dead from the humidity and heat so I inch along the heels of the woman in front of me who still has a dim light. We carry gifts and are dressed in our cleanest clothes. I had stuffed a washable, emerald green, silk blouse in my pack at the last moment. I smooth out the wrinkles with my hand and put on my favorite earrings with faux gems that sparkle. We are going to a party. The damp forest is more familiar now. I jerk as a crash of branches breaks beside us in the dark and two feet grab my ankles. My heart whirls and plunges ahead, but my feet are stuck. Two longhaired arms wrap around my chest and across my back.

"Apollo Bob!" I shout. "Get off me!"

The women turn back to help, dropping the gifts in the dirt, and swat about Bob's head and back.

"Let go. Let go."

I tip into the mud. Apollo Bob holds fast. I squirm but cannot budge against the grip of his powerful arms and legs. My mind flashes to my silk blouse that he is pawing.

"Don't rip my blouse, don't you dare rip my good blouse, Apollo Bob."

Without warning, he flees.

I take a hand to regain an upright posture. My blouse seems intact. My last pair of clean khakis are filthy. I brush them off anyway. We gather up our gifts and resume our march toward dinner. More astonished than afraid, my mind begins to challenge that this fleeting encounter actually happened. As we enter the clearing around the dining hut, galloping feet race across the dirt. Someone shrieks, "It's Apollo Bob!" In a flash he clamps my legs in the vice of his grip, releases, turns, and charges into the forest again. The Dayak men leap from their benches inside the building but Apollo Bob is gone before they can get out the door. This times my knees are shaking.

"My God, did he actually single me out?"

That night we gave speeches. Birute translated from Indonesian to English and English to Indonesian. We ate and exchanged gifts and drank warm Coca Cola. At 1:00 a.m. we were dancing to the Dayak drums. The only sign that remained was two, long, muddy, hand prints on the back of my green silk blouse and a question in my mind about how I would tell my husband that I was jumped by an orangutan named Apollo Bob.

SOMETHING IN THE AIR

ZONA SAGE

IT WAS SHORTLY AFTER TAKEOFF that I first noticed a sickening smell. "Do you smell that?" I asked my companion.

"Yes, what is it?" she scrunched her face in reaction to the odor.

"I don't know. Smells like bad kimchee, something like that?"

"No, I think methane, something chemical."

We were wedged into seats in the five-seat across middle section, with seats in front and in back of us. When the seats in front reclined, the jaws-of-life were necessary before we could get out to go to the bathroom. There was little room to move, much less to escape the awful smell invading the air.

The odor came in waves, getting worse at times. As the cart rolled down the aisle for our dinner, I mentioned the problem to the flight attendant doling out the dinner trays, a tall thin man with a curious tiny devil-like beard. I imagined him more at home in a black cape than his uniform.

"Yes, madam. We are aware of the problem. We believe that some passenger has brought cheese aboard and has it in an overhead bin. We'll check on it after dinner."

With no carry-on luggage to stuff into overhead bins, we had postponed the inevitable moment when the economy passengers would be stuffed into the storage areas they called our seats. With too many hours in transatlantic flight ahead on the fully booked flight from Paris to New York, we had savored the last few moments of wiggle room in the waiting area. We might have delayed even longer, had we known what awaited us on the flight.

Security was very tight at the Paris airport; especially as we were flying an American airliner, and terrorist concerns abounded. We submitted to a full security interrogation with passport and tickets before we were allowed to get into the ticket line to check our luggage. Where had we stayed? What had we done? How well did we know each other? Did we bring anything in our luggage at the request of anyone else? Had we packed our own suitcases?

After the ticket counter, we had to pass yet another security checkpoint with passports and boarding passes before we could ride the futuristic escalators that crisscrossed in see-through tubes in open space.

We cleared another security point (passports and boarding passes again) in order to proceed to our boarding gate. When we boarded the plane, we had to present our passports and boarding passes again. Even as we walked into the jetway that fed us onto the plane, uniformed personnel approached each of us separately. "May I see your passport?" "Did you buy anything at a duty-free shop?" "What did you buy?" "Do you have it with you?" I confessed to a small purchase of cologne and was released and allowed to board the plane at long last. I had never been through such tight security.

On the plane, hours went by. A disaster movie had played to conclusion; the earth had escaped complete annihilation when Robert Duvall sacrificed himself and his crew to crash into the oncoming meteor. The subsequent disaster called dinner had also played to conclusion, and I had survived that as well, possibly because I chose not to eat the mélange of pasta and melted plastic ("We apologize to those passengers whose food trays may have overheated.")

For some reason the stench had abated during dinner. After dinner, however, the malevolent odor returned and a huge nauseating wave of the smell attacked my senses. More people were complaining to the flight attendants about the stench. I stood by the galley with some other concerned passengers, trying to figure out what the smell was and where it was coming from. A gaggle of uniforms went up the aisles, placing their hands gingerly on the outside of the metal doors to the overhead compartments, as if feeling the temperature of the contents. "That's one test for it," I heard one say to another. A test for what? Was some vital airplane fluid leaking out? Were we going to burst into flames? I returned to my seat and put on my seat belt. Would we have to prepare for a crash landing? On my way back to my seat I noticed a Buddhist nun sitting peacefully right behind me, completely oblivious to the fuss and fury all around her. Ah, the bliss of a life devoted to more ethereal concerns.

"There, there it is, do you smell it?" One of the flight attendants was standing next to me in the aisle, talking to another. "God, it's horrible."

She was tall, with big wavy blonde hair and red lipstick. She seemed to be one of the senior fight attendants, and was maybe in her late 30s. She looked down at me. "Are you American?"

"Yes," I replied, thinking, Oh no, is terrorism involved?

"May I whisper in your ear?" She knelt down. "Do you think it could be the gentleman in front of you?"

I was taken aback. The older Asian man? Why would it be him? The flight attendant, on her knee at my side, didn't wait for my response. She bent forward slightly and sniffed at the back of the man. She looked at me, shook her head and got up.

The situation was obviously deemed serious by now, because a male from the cockpit was called upon to assist in tracking down the problem. After sniffing up and down the aisle, he was soon at my side. "Yes, I can smell it, " he told the female flight attendant who was apparently leading the search-and-destroy mission. "One of the flight attendants told me he thought it was cheese in an overhead bin up ahead," I volunteered to them, trying to be helpful.

A search commenced of the overhead bins, as one by one they were opened and the contents sniffed. No, it wasn't that.

"Excuse me." The petite, elegant Asian woman to my left was leaning toward me, talking very low. "I think the Vietnamese nun behind us, you know, she has brought on durian." Durian! The scourge of Asia, durian is a huge spiky fruit whose delights are prized by its devotees, driving its price up to great heights. Its reputation as an aphrodisiac helps some overcome the one big drawback to the fruit—its stench. Although its virtues are extolled, no one will deny the horrible stench, which has been compared to rotting flesh. Some have said eating durian is like eating strawberries and cream in a filthy outhouse. The smell is so horrible that signs are posted in hotel rooms and public conveyances throughout Asia: "No Durian Permitted."

I turned to the flight attendant at my right. "Have you traveled in Asia?" I asked her. "Yes, why?" I spoke only one word in reply. "Durian."

She recoiled. "My God, you're right! Durian!"

I relayed that the meek Buddhist nun directly behind me was suspected of having the dreaded fruit. The flight attendant went straight to the task.

"Durian?"

The nun turned over the contraband that she had succeeded in carrying through innumerable security checks: a large plastic container of the King of Fruit, as its fans call it. The flight attendant held it out ahead of her as she went forward with it. When the attendant returned without the dreaded package I plied her with questions.

"She said it was medicine, made from durian, that friends had given her," the flight attendant said. "She had it stored in that plastic container, and was eating it throughout the flight. So, whenever she took some out and ate it, the smell increased. She must have taken a dinner break, and then was back at it."

I wondered about the "medicinal" purposes of a fruit famed as an aphrodisiac. According to an Indonesian saying, "When the durian comes down, the sarongs go up." Was her "medicine" related to the blissed out state she seemed to be in?

We made the rest of the flight free from the noxious attack on our nostrils. But believe me, I am writing those folks at the Paris airport.

They are just not strict enough with those security checks.

Soup Kitchen

Edward Reed

Sometimes, the worldwide travel experience of a man's wife is worth more than you could ever believe. Having the opinion of a woman who has visited about 100 foreign counties may one day be important to you. It certainly should have been to me—if only I had listened to her!

In June 2004, on a journey to Croatia, and on the way to Dubrovnik via Bosnia-Herzegovina, our 54-passenger Insight tour bus was mired in heavy traffic. It became obvious we would not reach our planned lunch destination, so in desperation—and to alleviate the growing midday hunger pains of the group—the tour director stopped at a small grocery store where we could purchase snack and deli items for an impromptu meal. The tour group was forced to eat quickly, some of us standing up, at the side of the snarled roadway amid choking diesel fumes.

After traversing the Bosnia-Herzegovina border (no small task), we were all eager to get a nice bowl of hot soup, coffee or tea. On reaching the first outpost in Bosnia, the bus stopped again and I followed my wife Caroline into the first restaurant we could find, unaware that her interest was "emergency bathroom facilities." When my wife emerged from the bathroom, I, along with a South African couple, had secured a table for four. My wife came close enough to get my attention, motioned at me in her special way and whispered in a gentle voice, "Do not eat anything here!" After the South African gentleman ordered tomato soup, my wife repeated her admonition in a much higher pitched tone, "PLEASE . . . DO NOT EAT HERE."

Completely ignoring her warnings, and enjoying myself while listening to the travel adventures of our travel companions, I flagged-down the proprietor and ordered tomato soup myself. The menu was a little grubby-looking, torn. After ordering, I watched the gentleman who took our order squash a giant cockroach with the heel of his shoe . He did not spill a drop of the soup on the floor.

Then he and his wife suddenly decided to have a shouting match next to our table in their native language—Slavic. The soup, according to my wife, was dehydrated and reconstituted—made with water, not quite hot. Not exactly gourmet cooking in a country where we were told to drink bottled water!

Meantime, the proprietor and his wife, kept yelling at each other. We kept eating the soup. Suddenly the owner threw our U.S. coins out the front door while continuing to scream at his wife. In the middle of this domestic battle, they periodically stomped the dark brown critters running on the floor. A few of the roaches must have escaped because I remember hearing shrieks from across the room. My wife stood in the doorway dodging the coins that continued to fly her way.

The South Africans and I just ignored the restaurateurs, kept on talking and slurping down the tomato soup. Fortunately we arrived at our hotel room in Dubrovnik before the stomach cramps began, the 105-degree fever eroded my bedroom ambitions, the hallucinations and the seizure-like chills hit full blast. Speaking of hallucinations, this was the first time in my life that I can say that I saw green-colored snakes crawling on the ceiling of the hotel room (you know, the ten-foot-long kind, with their mouths open wide enough to get a large can of tomato soup in there). I lost five days and 15 meals—and all of Dubrovnik. Our tour guide suggested to my wife ". . . we ship the husband home alone" on an emergency flight.

However, the hotel came to our rescue and arranged for me to see a pretty young women doctor in Dubrovnik. The shot and the antibiotics she dispensed worked and I slowly returned from my near-death experience. When we arrived home a week later, it took more than a month for me to return to my previous "workaholic" self.

We blamed the tomato soup in Bosnia for my illness on the trip. That would be a fair guess. The moral of the story, as my wife likes to remind me, "Always listen to your wife, the experienced world traveler" before ordering tomato soup in Bosnia-Herzegovina.

When our cab left for the airport for the return trip home, the South African was still in his hotel room recovering from the soup—although, it could have been those dozen or so oysters he purchased from a roadside stand after the fisherman dug out each one from its shell with his pocket knife. Moreover, the South African did not make the going-away party the night before we left. Of course I was there, catching catnaps in my chair at the table most of the evening, dreaming about those green snakes moving around the hotel room ceiling.

In the Forest without a Dog

Andrew Grieser Johns

THE MOTOR CANOE GROUNDED ON THE SANDBANK with a jar that
pitched the bowman overboard into the shallow water.

"Where are we?" I asked.

"Just some stream or creek or something," said my assistant helpfully. "There aren't any maps."

There was a second splash as the fellow manning the high-
powered outboard engine also fell overboard, having been seriously depleting a private supply of cachaca (locally brewed
cane spirit) on the long journey upriver.

"If we lose him we're really stuck," I observed. He was
the only person who could work the engine and I couldn't
remember having seen any paddles in the canoe.

"We," intoned one of my fellow scientists seriously, "are
in the forest without a dog."

"Portuguese idiom," explained my assistant. "And don't
put your foot in the water, there'll be piranhas."

"They didn't touch the two who already fell in."

"They're from Parana."

"So, what do we do now?"

"Try getting out of the boat for a start. And tread carefully. There'll be stingrays."

"So how do we know this is the right place?"

"This is where the boatman brought us. So it must be right."

My assistant leapt athletically over the side of the canoe and disappeared to his waist in an underwater pothole that might have been excavated by an electric eel. If it was, its owner either wasn't at home or figured that cariocas were already sufficiently hyperactive. He gained the bank undamaged.

I followed rather carefully.

We were somewhere off the Tocantins River in eastern Brazilian Amazonia. The Tocantins is a big river. The flow can be 89,000 cubic yards per second at flood levels. Its annual outflow is greater than that of the Mississippi: half as much as the Zaire River. It is the most easterly of the major tributaries that flow north from the central Brazilian shield and eventually merge to make up the Amazon River itself. It is full of bizarre and little-known creatures, many of which bite, and meanders through one of the largest remaining areas of rain forest in eastern Amazonia.

The reason for our presence was an expedition to investigate the ecological impact of a major Amazonian hydroelectric project. It was March 1984. An enormous dam was being built across the Tocantins River at Tecurui. Rather late in the day, the hydroelectric company had realized that some assessment was required about the impact of a 1,000-square-mile lake in what was previously undisturbed forest. A group of Brazilian and overseas scientists had been contracted to undertake baseline surveys of the animals inhabiting the forest in the lake region.

I had been conducting surveys of various types of animals in different parts of the world for some years and the technical aspects in the current job didn't bother me. I did have some worries about the time allocated to cover the land area involved. Generally, however, I counted myself fortunate to be in such an exotic and exciting place.

I had been telling myself this quite a lot during the three-day delay in Tecurui while we were waiting for transport to materialize. Tecurui was a typical ramshackle Amazonian boomtown, grown up over a few years to serve the needs, mainly liquid and/or biological, of the construction workers. Apart from such high spots as The Cockroach Bar/Restaurant on the main street, where cold beer was to be had, generally accompanied by the unwelcome attentions of the resident transvestites in which this particular place seemed to specialize, the town had little to offer. All such towns seem to have establishments called The Cockroach, or even The Giant Cockroach. I was told it merely signifies a good place to be: Brazilian cockroaches are a bit picky.

When we finally embarked on the first trip upriver the feeling of general excitement returned. The mud-laden waters of the river were at flood levels. The river was several miles wide and fast flowing, dotted with clinging clumps of vegetation that marked submerged sandbars. Dead trees and other debris swirled past, smaller pieces hitting the boat with dull thuds before vanishing in our wake. Waterbirds abounded: large-billed terns with Concorde profiles dived for small fry in the shallows, herons and egrets flapped into trees at the river margins, ospreys wheeled overhead. The Amazonian touch was provided by occasional flights of macaws and parrots, which passed overhead calling raucously. Leaving our companion boats straggling in line behind, we lost ourselves in the muddy vastness that is the Amazon basin.

Back to reality, I trudged up the sandy beach, already slapping vigorously at the biting sand flies. The boatman, shouting down from a vantage point, informed us that we were in the correct place and could start unloading. Other motor canoes began appearing from downriver. More victims for the sand flies, the head-shrinking Indians, or whatever else lurked in the dense forest I could vaguely see through the haze of mosquitoes hovering over the neighborhood swamp.

As the canoes pulled up on the beach, researchers from all over Brazil began to mill around aimlessly, giving the place the aura of a scientific congress. The more practical laborers began putting up what was to be the first of several tented encampments at various points down the 100-mile stretch of the Tocantins that would disappear within the lake. A completed encampment consisted of two or three huge tarpaulins erected over sturdy poles and covering a framework for slinging hammocks. That was the sleeping area. Several smaller shelters acted as laboratory or work areas and as the kitchen, although these were often undistinguishable. The kitchen, which was generally erected at the best vantage point, inevitably became the acknowledged social area, and the site of some fascinating gastronomical experimentation.

We, the assembled company, represented the first phase of the Ticurui Wildlife Project: the research operation. Our role was to document the numbers of animals within the rain forest that would end up beneath the lake. As the lake flooded, we pointy-headed scientists would be replaced by the much more macho animal-grabbers who would be implementing the animal-rescue phase: "Operation Curupira." (The rescue operation was named, incidentally, after a mythical, pestilential little beast with its feet on backwards, whose ostensible role is that of spirit guardian of forest animals but which, as any hunter will tell you, is all too easily seduced away from its purpose by strong drink.)

What made the preliminary research operation attractive at all, to most people, was the provision of a substantial per diem for participants. Researchers fought for places. Encampments swarmed with entomologists; writhed with herpetologists; were plagued with epidemiologists. I and my assistant, who were interested in live animals in situ, rather than specimens or component parts thereof in petri dishes, were in something of a minority. The general feeling was that since the animals in the lake area were doomed anyway, it was a chance to forget whatever moral scruples you might ever have had and push forward in the name of Science. The sight of entomologists setting off with chainsaws to collect canopy insects might have seemed a little extreme, but it undoubtedly saved a lot of time and trouble climbing trees. I could see the reasoning, but unlike most Brazilian researchers I was not an aspiring amateur hunter. My assistant and I were in the forest for much of the day, and occasionally part of the night too, and saw a great many animals, from snakes to jungle cats. But I had no particular wish to grab, trap or shoot them, or to allow my assistant to do so. Amongst the cytogeneticists, my name was mud.

There is a well-known saying that perhaps originated among the Somalis of the horn of Africa. It runs something like "Those who know it, do it; those who know a little, teach it; those who know nothing, direct it." Within an hour of our arrival, several distinguished scientists were arguing furiously with the laborers over the correct way to erect the kitchen. Leaving them to it, I coaxed my assistant away from the array of shotguns, which he was eying appreciatively, and we started walking around the periphery of the campsite to take stock of our surroundings. I did not like the look of the swamp. It seemed that we were setting ourselves up on an island isolated from the terra-firma forest. No one else seemed concerned. A couple of herpetologists wandered along the edge of the swamp in the other direction looking for snakes that might already be moving away from the site of disturbance. In the shade of a clump of trees, the entomologists were settling down for an afternoon nap. The cook had already borrowed a shotgun and was busy shooting at hawks that were sitting watching the proceedings. My assistant and I set off to try and find a way through the swamp. It had alligators in it.

Some time later, having got lost and been forced to splash around in the dark for an hour or so, we emerged again, relatively unscathed. The company was assembled in the newly erected kitchen eating dinner. The cook had organized his domain and produced something quite pleasant from meat brought upriver. There wouldn't be much more of that, so we made the most of it. What we were going to eat in the meantime, I had no idea. I supposed that the cook would think of something.

"Pirarara," said the ichthyologist, in answer to a somewhat tentative inquiry. "It's a kind of carnivorous catfish. They grow really big and there are stories of people being dragged down into the depths by them. Could happen: look at those teeth. This one is actually quite interesting. It might even be a new subspecies. Have some."

He continued eating it reflectively.

It was very good. I had seen a lot worse lately. I even felt friendly toward the cook. It was a relief generally to get back to camp—be it ever so humble.

Together with my assistant I had spent the previous two weeks at a hunting station some way upriver, where I had been looking for some of the rare monkeys that were to be found in that region. The menu there had consisted of boiled tortoise twice a day. The giant forest tortoises were anything up to about thirty-inches long and had a habit of sunning themselves in the middle of forest trails. With my eyes on the canopy, I was forever falling over them. It wouldn't have immediately occurred to me to eat them, although I understand that there are Indian tribes that eat very little else and thrive on it. There is nothing quite like getting up at dawn on a chill, damp morning and facing cold boiled tortoise for breakfast.

One of the herpetologists wandered in with a small, diamond-patterned snake, which he casually dropped in a bucket by my feet.

"The Indians call this one a 'tenstep,'" he remarked informatively. "They say that if it bites you, you can generally walk about ten steps before dropping dead. Tell me if it moves."

He helped himself to some carnivorous catfish.

I put my feet up on the bench.

The ornithologist, who had arrived on the latest boat, dropped her plate and rushed outside as screeching from the trees indicated that the golden-winged parakeets were back. These small, green, yellow-winged parrots were generally believed to be endangered, but the riverine forest around that part of the Tocatins were full of them. I had seen several groups of them in the riverine forest adjacent to the hunting station. I had also seen a number of other rare species. Most spectacular among them were hyacinth macaws: massive purple birds, the largest of the parrot family and increasingly rare as a result of the pet trade.

I told this to the ornithologist after she returned from counting the local group of parakeets. She thought that the riverine forests in the area might be a staging post for the species during its annual migration, which would explain the high density of the birds.

She pushed plates, salt, and boxes of insects out of the way to write some notes, then walked over to the food and peered into another pot the cook had just brought in.

The cook was the final recipient of any specimens that came into camp, being last in line after the epidemiologists and the taxidermist. As in the most exclusive of London clubs, you never knew quite what would appear on the table, only that it would have a sauce over it. Even before I had left for the hunting station, armadillos, porcupines, and other large rodents, howler, bearded saki and white-fronted capuchin monkeys all put in an appearance at one time or another. The last was particularly unpleasant.

During my absence, the cook had surprised everyone, however, by displaying distinctly human emotions. He had befriended a large and extremely spiky iguana that would come into the back of the kitchen for scraps. Unfortunately, a collector who had arrived on the same boat as the ornithologist had not been told in time and the iguana now reposed in a tub of fermol. The cook was not happy and had been sharpening his cleaver in a threatening manner. That was the end of his flirtation with the rest of humanity.

I went to get some water from the tank, the filters being empty.

"Watch your fingers," said the herpetologist, collecting the tenstep and its bucket. "There's a snapping turtle in there."

I recalled that when I left it had been piranhas.

From beside the water tank I watched curiously as a Gordian knot on two legs staggered past the kitchen enroute to the laboratory tent. The herpetologist, tenstep and bucket also came to watch.

"Is that you?" he asked eventually, perhaps recognizing his colleague's feet. "Need some help with that boa constrictor?"

For the next few weeks I wanted to stay around the main camp to work in forest on the west bank of the river, accessible only by water canoe. In this part of the Amazon Basin, the terra-firma forests were tall, but uneven, with many gaps containing lower, almost impenetrable vegetation. Most of the large emergent trees, rising above the rest of the canopy, were Brazil-nut trees, whose cannonball fruit littered the ground underneath them. ("Brazil nuts," as sold in the supermarket, are actually seeds: each fruit contains many of these, surrounded by a hard outer casing and weighing about three-and-a-half pounds. Not something you want to fall on your head.)

The undergrowth in the forest was rich in spiny palms and various shrubs with associated ant colonies. I was constantly amazed at how many ants there were in Amazonia compared with elsewhere in the tropics. And some had extremely painful bites. Cutting trails through the forest I was constantly bitten by ants, which swarmed over my arms as I pushed vegetation aside, or dropped down my neck from overhanging branches. There were plenty of wasps, too.

Professionally, I was more interested in larger animals, particularly the primates. We had already found the rare bearded saki monkey on the east bank and wanted to compare population densities on either side of the river. This monkey is medium-sized and rather skinny underneath a coarse fur coat, and has a curiously shaped head with large bumps on the top of the skull. This is caused by an eccentric jaw musculature, necessary for the job of cracking the hard seeds on which the monkey specializes. Working with them wasn't easy: they are very wide-ranging animals and were encountered only rarely during the surveys. We started to accumulate some information, however, and began to notice morphological differences between the populations on the different banks of the river. We failed to find the even rarer white-whiskered spider monkeys, which supposedly reach the western bank of the Tocantins. Of the numerous hunters we interviewed, only one remembered seeing them some way inland twenty years previously. Not a common animal.

Working out of the camp was more difficult than sitting out in a hunting station. Transport across the river was not always as punctual as might be desired, for one thing. However, the chance to socialize a little at breakfast and dinner was welcome. Conversation in the kitchen tent was invariably interesting and often enlightening. In the spirit of camaraderie through shared hardship (capuchin monkey, for instance), you sometimes learned the secret dreams of your fellow scientists.

The leader of the team of epidemiologists came into the kitchen one evening and sat down with a sigh.

"I had a terrible day," he said. "Nothing was diseased at all. And I had a terrible night last night, too. Partly due to that capybara and partly due to my recurring nightmare."

The reference to a capybara arose from a sighting of that largest of rodents on the edge of camp the previous midnight. The beast, which is the size of a large pig, had been busily getting its distinctly roman nose into the vegetables outside the kitchen, But the cook, ever protective of his onions, had spotted it. Visions of capybara steaks doubtlessly foremost in his mind, he had screamed a warning.

Never have I seen scientists out of their hammocks so fast. First into the swamp were the cytogeneticists; the epidemiologists and herpetologists tied for second. By the time I had extricated myself, being less familiar with hammocks, the swamp was half-full of scientists in various brightly colored items of underwear. All were splashing around in circles, shining lights into one another's eyes and shouting incomprehensibly. The capybara escaped. One of the herpetologists managed to grab a largish alligator, or vice versa. The entomologists slept through it.

"In this dream," the epidemiologist continued, "I've just died. I go through the Pearly Gates and there, in front of me, are rows and rows of animals. Big ones, little ones, adult ones, baby ones. All the animals we've killed for leishmaniasis screening over the years. They're all pointing at me and screaming, 'It was him! It was him!' So down I go, down into the pit. The external torment . . ."

He shrugged and peered into the stew, a haunted man. He ladled out a few spoonfuls of his latest victim.

As we progressed through the time allotted for our research efforts, we moved slowly south through the lake area. The forest varied little, but the floods that forced us to wade chest deep through muddy water at the start of our morning surveys, holding binoculars and notebook over our heads, gradually receded. As the waters went down, vast expanses of blinding white sand were uncovered. To get from the access points of the river into our study areas we then had to spend hours baking in the reflected heat, following the meandering sandbars towards the terra-firma forests. It would have been much quicker to wade through the many inlets that cut the sandbars into a mosaic of interconnecting strips, but having noticed the three-foot-long, blue-spotted stingrays that buried themselves in the fine sand in the deeper water, I was disinclined to try. So we picked our way through the sandbar maze, eyes almost closed against the glare, disturbing the nesting terns, and frightening groups of black skimmers.

Over time, we began to get clear estimates of the numbers of animals that would be displaced by the formation of the lake. The numbers were considerable. We did not know, of course, how many would manage to swim from the flooding area to the margins, or how many would persist on the many small islands that would remain in the lake. But it was certain that many would drown, and also that the overcrowding at the margin and on the islands would eventually lead to starvation, or death through fighting and other stresses, of many more. Only predators could be expected to benefit, and even these, only in the short term.

That one of the last remaining large patches of forest in the region should be lost through flooding, and through associated developments, was tragic. But Brazil needed the hydroelectric power to support industry to generate foreign currency to service its foreign debt. Western banks financed the construction of the dam, perhaps to ensure the growth of the industrial base that would support the debt service.

Global politics was far above us, however, as we thrashed about in the undergrowth amidst the monkeys and herds of peccaries. Our role was to document the process. Perhaps our findings would be relevant to the many other hydroelectric projects that were being planned at that time. There had been many plans for harnessing the hydroelectric generative potential of the Amazon, from an international think tank's scheme to dam the Amazon itself east of Manaus, to Brazil's own "Plane 2010," which called for eighty separate dams flooding a total area of 39,000 square miles. (Sounds like a lot, but that's actually only 2 percent of the extant forest area.) Under that scheme the Tocantins would be spanned by seven large and twenty smaller dams, turning it into a chain of lakes 1,200 miles long. Development on a large scale, indeed.

Our final camp was located on a large island, some six miles long and three wide, in the middle of the Tocantins River itself. It forced the entire flow of the river into two sets of impressive rapids, in places only 20 to 30 yards wide and most exhilarating to navigate in a motor canoe. I spent the last few days sitting amidst the sandflies, above the beach, writing up notes. We had documented several variations among the monkeys, one of which would later be separated into a new subspecies, extended the known geographical range of several large mammals and located important populations of several rare birds. Various colleagues had discovered a new species of snake and a vast number of new insects, especially ants. Important reference collections had been made. Bales of skin and crates of bottles, snakes and pinned insects were heading for various museums around the world that would work on them. It would take many years to sort out precisely what had been discovered. By that time, the Ticurui forests would be long gone, of course.

The expedition drew to a close, with the pooling of data and last-minute collection of interesting animal groups.

"Pomarine ants," said the head of the entomology group informatively.

I had arrived back from the forest just in time for lunch and had thought that the plastic box on the rough plank table had something edible in it.

I slammed the lid back on, stopping most of its centimeter-long biting inhabitants from swarming out onto my rice and beans. Since the collecting was now largely complete, the kitchen fare had become less varied.

A bit farther down the table an opaque plastic bag was revolving slowly around a tin containing spare knives and forks. Its curious perambulations suggested a bird-eating spider, but I didn't like to ask.

A herpetologist came into the kitchen tent for a glass of water and began sprinkling it over a small knot of gently writhing snakes lying gasping in a tin tray.

"Heatstroke," he explained, as he walked off with them.

"Pomarine ants," the entomologist continued, "are most interesting creatures. Unfortunately, their taxonomy is very confused. The 19th-century taxonomist made a poor job of it, even by the standard of the times. He would forget where he was in the trays, come back after lunch and reclassify whole series of ants again in a completely different way. Hopeless. The group has just been revised extremely well, based on features of coloration of the thorax and abdomen. They fall into distinct groups. A divergent specimen has never been found, so the keying out of specimens is quite easy.

A small, undistinguished-looking pomarine ant, which had crawled up onto the table from near the entrance to the tent, chose that moment to make a dash for the sugar bowl.

"Take this specimen, for instance," the entomologist said, picking it up and looking at it through a hand lens.

He put it down again and squashed it with his coffee mug.

Outside, various scientists were playing a game, which involved guessing the weight of a boa constrictor that had drowned in one of the fish traps and which went off the end of the herpetologists' scales.

"I want an accurate guess," one of them was saying belligerently. "This is scientific research, not a fairground."

The following day they collapsed the kitchen tent. That was the effective end of the expedition.

The Ticurui dam was closed at the end of September. Our work in the area had lasted about seven months. We handed over to the animal rescue team. "Operation Curupira" swung into action, complete with helicopters, international film crews, and medical teams to deal with the people who grabbed the wrong sort of snake. Between September and the following April, some 20,000 monkeys were fished out of the rising waters, as were sundry other beasts, including over 25,000 bird-eating spiders. Some thirty million U.S. dollars were spent along the way.

Most of the animals drowned in the lake, nonetheless. Even the 470 people involved couldn't cover the whole area. Most animals that were captured were released on islands or at the lake margin, where most probably starved or were killed by the hunters that flocked to the scene. Generally unnoticed amidst the excitement, that particular piece of the Amazonian rain forest slowly disappeared.

No one fished any curupiras from the lake. Perhaps they can swim.

Pining Away

Janet Roberts

My PARENTS WERE VISITING and we had just the ticket, a meal aboard a dinner train that would take us into Michigan's backwoods. Shortly after the train pulled out, our salad was served and I felt a strange sensation in my mouth, right after I touched the dressing to my lips (I have been plagued with a food allergy for years). Then my sister noticed my voice was getting huskier by the moment. My quick-thinking husband asked if I had brought my bee-sting kit with me.

After giving me an initial shot, he immediately found a steward and asked for an ambulance. Then he took me back to the restroom to administer a second shot.

Since the women's room was occupied, my husband pushed me into the men's room for the second shot. By now, people were noticing something was wrong—particularly when the train came to a halt at a railroad crossing and the wail of an approaching ambulance could be heard in the distance.

The rest of my family remained on the train while we disembarked. As we waited for the emergency medical technicians, a dozen small-town residents tipped off by their scanners, pulled up. The first responder was the local fire department. They had no idea what to do about the fact that my throat was swelling shut. My husband suggested oxygen might prove helpful. But their attention appeared to be focused on the approaching ambulance. They were worried about losing this new case. I was beginning to feel like a piece of road kill.

As the ambulance arrived the hangers-on, disappointed by the lack of blood, drifted way. My husband insisted that I be taken to the hospital immediately. But the driver insisted that I be stabilized first. My husband offered to drive while the EMT worked on me, but regulations were against it. Finally, I was packed into the ambulance, and siren blaring, down the road we went until our path was blocked by a slow-moving freight train. The driver advised the hospital about our delay as he swung the ambulance around and took another road. We were stopped at a second crossing by the same train. The ambulance took another detour.

When we finally pulled up to the emergency area of the hospital, the entire staff was waiting just for ME! I spent the next three days in intensive care. I did find out the source of my food allergy—a small pine nut.

Bulgogi to Die For

Hemlata Vasavada

It was my husband, Nitin's, search for bulgogi and kimchi in Kaneohe, Hawaii that got me in trouble. He wanted to eat the beef dish he had tasted in Korea twenty years earlier. Our friend, Karuna, took us to a Korean restaurant. While we sipped glasses of iced tea, my picky husband explored the menu.

He complained, "This bulgogi is not barbecued. Let's try the diner across the street."

Following the garlicky barbecue aroma we entered the diner. After placing my orders I headed for the facilities.

I stepped into a restroom slightly bigger than a plane's toilet. On my way out, I realized the doorknob wasn't working. I rattled and jiggled the knob, then pulled and pushed it hoping the pin would make contact. No such luck. I pounded the door, waited and banged again. At least some air was coming from the ventilator. But no way could I climb up and get out that small opening.

Surely my companions would notice my absence and rescue me. Finally after fifteen minutes that seemed like hours, I heard Karuna. "Hema, are you in there?"

Now where else would I be? "I'm trapped."

She tried turning the knob. The metal clanked. The knob rotated. It didn't open. She assured me, "Don't worry, we'll get you out in a minute. Nitin, Hema is locked in. Waiter, please help us."

A man pushed and twisted the knob. A promising "clank," then nothing.

Several voices on the far side of the barrier advised the man. "Turn this way. No, try to push it in and turn."

Nitin called, "Hem, are you okay?"

I rolled my eyes. "Yes," I managed to say.

"You must call a locksmith," Nitin told them.

"But we need the owner's permission. She should be coming soon," someone said.

Nitin asked me, "Do you have your credit card?"

I clutched my purse. " Do we have to pay the locksmith in advance?"

"No. Slide the card in the door by the lock," Nitin suggested.

Remembering how the burglars opened locks in the movies, I tried to slide my card. There was no space between the door and the doorframe. "It won't fit."

From the crowd someone asked, "Can you breathe?"

Didn't she hear me huffing? "Yes, I'm okay."

Another voice inquired, "How old is she?"

I clenched my fists. They probably thought I was crazy. It's okay for a child to get locked up, but for a mature adult to be in this situation! What if my two-year-old grandson had been in this cubbyhole? I shivered in the heat as perspiration trickled down my temples.

More questions from strangers. "Is she claustrophobic? Any medical problems? Call 911."

I stood by the door, awaiting rescue, listening to voices amid the symphony of hammers and screeching metals, and thought of the novel I was reading. I should have brought along *One Hundred Years of Solitude.* Thinking about the character in the book, who had to live in a room full of chamber pots, made me giggle. How ironic!

Pounding hammers and grating screwdrivers assaulted my ears. "We have removed the door hinges," Nitin told me. "The door is still lodged in the doorframe. You have to push from inside."

I applied my five-foot, one-hundred-pound might on the door. It didn't budge.

"Use force," Nitin ordered.

Had the "Force" been with me, I would have beamed myself out long ago. My legs trembled. I wanted to sit down. But the toilet didn't have a lid and I didn't want to get caught sitting on the commode when the door opened. I could slump on the floor, but worried that if the men kept hammering, the door might fall and squish me like a dead cockroach on the floor.

Finally, Nitin pried the door open. He gave me a hug and went to wash his greasy hands in the doorless toilet. I faced the cheering diners, as if the curtain had just up on my one woman show. My face burnt. I wanted to cover my head and slink away.

Karuna embraced me. "What an ordeal!"

Another customer said: "Look, you're perspiring. Who wouldn't in that cubbyhole? Put a cold cloth on your forehead."

I took out my hanky and wiped my face, pretending it was no big deal.

"You're a saint," Karuna complimented me. "I would have screamed bloody murder. I even thought of calling a lawyer."

"And ask him to bring his burglar-client to break the lock?"

Forty minutes later, when we returned to our table, Nitin's bulgogi had turned leathery and Karuna's "sizzling tofu" had lost its pizzazz. They had also forgotten my kimchi.

The waitress brought me a big glass of Coke. "On the house," she said.

Nitin mumbled, "Just a Coke? At least they could have given us free kimchi."

Stranger in Paradise

Linda Wasylenko

WHEN MY LUGGAGE DIDN'T SHOW UP on the airport baggage carousel, I had a feeling my trip to the Dominican Republic was not going to be something to write home about. Since it was very hot and the only clothes I had were the long pants and shirt I was wearing, I stuck close to my air-conditioned room. My husband put on his swim trunks and with a "you're sure you don't mind?" headed down to the beach.

The hotel staff reassured me that the wayward luggage would arrive any minute. Of course there were no clothing shops at the resort and I was now stuck with a single outfit. Two days later, with no luggage in sight, I decided to go shopping in the nearby town. The hotel reluctantly arranged for a taxi to take me into town the next morning. They warned that it was a dangerous place for tourists.

Although the resort was luxurious the town was crowded, dirty and dilapidated. A beat-up convertible passed through the streets with a man standing in the back seat, angrily shouting to the crowd through a megaphone. It looked as if the revolution would be starting any second. Although our cab waited to take us back to the resort, we needed to stay in town long enough for me to find a clothing store.

Eager to avoid revolutionary politics, we began moving away from the protest. As soon as we were out of sight, two men began following us. One actually felt my husband's arms and shoulders and said, "You seem like a pretty strong guy." The other man silently followed closely behind us as we tried to find a shop where I could buy something to wear. The larger man who was now blocking our way insisted he could help. "Send your cab away," he said, "I'll take you around and get you back to your hotel." He tried steering us toward a side street insisting he knew a jewelry factory where we could get discount prices. I declined but he persisted, as the other man continued to follow up.

Trying to escape, we hurried into the nearest shop. They waited patiently outside. I bought a few things and then we ran down the street toward the waiting cab, a few steps ahead of our new friends. Like hungry lions, they watched as we drove away.

It was a relief to get back to the resort even though the promised luggage still had not arrived. After dinner I began feeling ill and spent the night in the bathroom. By morning, my stomach was entirely empty. I was exhausted and weak. Unable to hold down water, I stayed in bed and sucked on ice cubes. The hotel doctor prescribed medication for my gastro-intestinal problem and I spent the next few days in bed while my husband played tennis, parasailed, swam, snorkeled, etc. Every so often he would pop in to let me know how bad he felt for me, and then he was off again. The fact that he was having a good time made me feel worse.

The day before we were due to leave, I finally felt a little better. I was determined to wear at least one of the new outfits I had purchased trip. Feeling weak dizzy and determined, I put on a beautiful white dress with eyelet lace trim. We chose an outdoor table at the hillside restaurant to enjoy the view and the lovely breeze. Still unable to eat, I sipped a ginger ale and suddenly noticed my new white dress was covered with little black spots.

My husband immediately explained the problem. Apparently after harvesting their sugar cane crop, farmers burn their fields. The beautiful breeze brought the cane ashes up from the valley farms. My dress was ruined. Tears were now streaming down my sooty face. This holiday was officially over.

When we finally arrived back in Buffalo, there was a big surprise at the airport. After a great deal of effort the airline had actually managed to locate my missing bags and send them home. Unfortunately my husband's bags were unaccounted for.

Thoroughly exhausted, still feeling queasy and dizzy, I sat down on the floor and leaned against the wall to wait while my husband filed a lost luggage report. A woman and a little boy were standing a few feet away. The child came over and looked down at me, "You are a poopy, poopy lady!" he shouted. His mother immediately ran over and grabbed his arm, apologizing profusely to me. I shook my head saying, "No, no, it's all right, the child is absolutely right. I am a poopy, poopy lady." The woman quickly backpedaled while warning her son about the dangers of talking to strangers. As we drove out of the airport parking lot my husband turned to me with a huge smile on his suntanned face and asked "So, where do you want to go next year?"

Eating At The Ritz

Dawn Starin

Like most field workers, I follow an incredibly disciplined schedule. On a personal level, I run like a well-oiled machine. Every morning I get up, make a cup of vacuum-packed instant coffee, eat my Scottish oats, slip on my British wellies, pack my lunch of locally produced boiled eggs, bananas and cashew nuts, strap on my knapsack and leave for the forest.

I make one entire round checking out the trees where the red colobus monkeys sleep and, of course, looking for snakes—my absolutely favorite animals—and then stay with one colobus troop. It rarely varies, and it doesn't bore me. I can sit for hours watching the colobus do nothing, absolutely nothing, something they are experts at. And, although I like to pretend that I am in control of my days, it is the colobus who actually decide where I go and what I do. Being such a control freak outside the forest, maybe this is the one time when I let another force take over and organize my life. Maybe I actually enjoy letting go and giving up responsibility—but only to the non-human aspect of this world. There is no way I can even pretend to control my days once I enter the forest. The forest has rules of its own and they must be obeyed.

Like most field workers, my days are early and full of amazing sites and sights. My thoughts and dreams are full of the animals I study. And, unfortunately, my diet is generally boring. I usually live on locally produced food, canned goods—mostly tomato paste and baked beans—and the goodies I scrounge when I go to eat at the better-paid, higher-up-the-food-chain, homes.

Sometimes, however, I need, I crave, the luxury of sitting down in a restaurant, looking at a menu, making decisions and having someone cook for me. Sometimes I need to slink off. Sometimes I simply need to rebel.

And so, today, being hot and hungry and tired, I decide to leave the forest early and eat at a very basic, local restaurant. Chipped tins plates, cracked glasses, dirty plastic tablecloth. It's fine. They have a menu; I have choices. I'm ecstatic. I love it. When I sit down, the waiter and I exchange greetings. "Hello, how's the day?" "How is your family?" "How is your work?" "Are you well?" "No pain in the body?" He hands me a glass of cold water and asks if I would like to read today's newspaper while I wait for my meal. I am gobsmacked. The Gambia possesses one of the highest illiteracy rates in Africa—more than 52 percent of the males and 67 percent of the females over age 15 cannot read or write, so to be handed a newspaper by a waiter is something quite out of the ordinary.

After I finish my peppery, fresh tomato, carrot, onion and lettuce salad, homemade chips and spicy vegetable stew, the best meal I have had in weeks, the waiter and the cook invite me to try some of their domada—rice, peanut paste and spicy meat stew. When I explain that I am a vegetarian, the cook explains that Gambians don't have those options. "We can't choose what we eat. We eat what we have grown up with, what our mothers gave us, what we can afford, what is good for us." And he's right. I have never seen a child here throw a hissy fit and complain about a meal. I have never heard anyone say "Yuck. I'm not eating this. It's disgusting." And the food is good and good for you. Like food throughout the tropics, Gambian food is spicy and contains lots of natural antimicrobials to ward off pathogens and parasites—a necessary requirement in this disease-riddled land.

While we sit discussing ingredients and market prices, a Rasta friend of theirs walks into the restaurant complaining of malaria. The cook walks outside, picks some leaves from a tree and boils them in water. He gives this concoction to his friend tells him to drink it three times a day and the malaria will disappear. Turning to me, he says, "We are dying like shit from malaria, and people have to start taking the medicines they can afford. The trees give us that." Again, I am stunned. I'm glad I held my own little personal rebellion. I know that I will return again and again for this fine food and extraordinary wisdom.

My Family, Food and Fieldwork

A. Magdalena Hurtado

FIELDWORK AMONG PEOPLE WHOSE BEHAVIOR and ideas about the world differ greatly from our own cannot only be a very funny experience but also a revealing one. We enter a new social and belief systems with misplaced and unrealistic behavioral expectations of ourselves, and of the people we hope to befriend. Frequently, we merely watch, and learn a great deal about people's social preferences, concerns, ideas, feelings and worldviews.

I have spent thirty-three months in the field. I did most of my earlier fieldwork with a friend (Hillard Kaplan) and my husband (Kim Hill) and later, with our daughter (Karina) as well. We've worked with lowland South America indigenous peoples, mainly the Ache of eastern Paraguay and the Hiwi of southwestern Venezuela, who depend on foraging for their sustenance to varying extremes, and for whom food is an obsession. Food became my obsession as well, and learning how to satisfy my cravings ironically taught me a great deal about

142

how married women manage to procure meat from men in these societies.

In addition to food, social relationships are also an obsession for the Ache and Hiwi, as is probably the case in all societies. I found that becoming socially competent under field conditions is almost impossible, due to the demands of data collection and numerous other self-sustenance tasks one needs to accomplish. However, I made every attempt to attain at least a level of social competency that could be tolerated by the people we lived with.

The Ache are a lot of fun. They love to laugh, tell jokes, tickle one another, and show physical affection in many ways. It is not at all uncommon to find Ache sitting very close to one another, spontaneously cleaning insects off each other's bodies, and feeling quite at ease with physical contact. Up to that point in my life, I was under the misconception that the Venezuelan culture I had grown up in had reduced individuals' immediate spatial boundaries to a minimum. The Ache eliminated that last bit of space.

The Ache were traditionally hunter-gatherers. We worked with a band that had settled over the course of the 1970s in an agricultural settlement, and depended on corn, sweet manioc, and store-bought goods for much of their subsistence. However, they frequently left the settlement to hunt and gather in the surrounding forests.

The events I am about to describe took place during my first visit to the Ache in 1981. We lived with this band over a period of nine months in foraging camps comprised of three to seven families. We stayed in these camps for weeks and months at a time, and spent very few days at the agricultural settlement. These were my most interesting experiences because I spent so much time in the forest.

Because Kim had lived several years with the Ache prior to my first visit, it was relatively easy becoming "socially accepted." Being associated with Kim was certainly not enough, however. The Ache watched me very closely to see if I learned to do things the Ache way, and when my mastery of skills was flawed they ridiculed me with delight. It took a while, but I finally learned to laugh at my awkwardness since no matter how hard I tried, I simply couldn't do such simple tasks such as gathering firewood, starting a fire, keeping a fire going, and cooking efficiently.

On my first foraging trip, I had a very vague notion of what to expect. I knew that we would probably wake up before dawn every day, start walking to our new camp not much later, and arrive sometime between two and six in the afternoon.

I was worried about stepping on snakes, falling off makeshift bridges, or losing my data notebooks or pens. I wondered if I could survive an unpredictable number of days eating monkeys, peccaries, armadillos, palm larvae, palm starch and other foods I had never tried before. On that first day I made friends with an older Ache woman. She stayed with me, and this made me feel secure. I opportunistically chose her as my focal person (the individual whose behavior I would sample over that entire day). By using her, I violated an important rule in data collection: sampling individuals at random. It turned out that this violation of protocol was insignificant compared to all the other biases I introduced during those first days. I collected less data when gnats and mosquitoes turned writing into torture, and collected still less, if any, data when we stood under the hot sun and sweaty hands made my Bic pens useless. Eventually I learned to avoid these problems by wearing several layers of clothing when the weather was bad, by keeping my data notebook in a small plastic bag, and by using a handkerchief frequently to dry my hands. The initial data were so poor that we had to exclude them from all our analysis.

My memories of foraging trips are imbued with hunger. I always felt as if I didn't have enough food; and I could never tell when I would get it. Between bouts of data collection I would often think about data collection and a handful of nuts I had hidden in my knapsack for an after-dark meal.

By the second day, I had eaten most of the candy I had brought and tried to convince Kim and Hilly to give me theirs without success (we each kept a few hidden in our daypacks). Consequently, that evening I was so hungry that I managed to eat monkey meat even though the night before I wouldn't take a single bite.

That night I learned that when a woman is accompanied by her husband, she is not given meat directly, but is expected to share with her spouse. Kim had spent the day with a hunter who decided to return to camp at dusk. There were a few who had returned earlier in the afternoon, meat had been cooked and several people were eating. I had to wait until dark to eat, and not until after Kim had bathed. Up to that point I had been very happy about the benefits of having a spouse in the field, not realizing that when it came to meat, husbands could be a liability for women; the few, single women in our foraging trips were shared with directly and plentifully, but not me. As I quickly ate a piece of armadillo I had hoped to eat hours ago, I wondered about the generalization one often hears in introductory anthropology courses: that food is equally shared in hunting and gathering societies.

I was much more preoccupied with food than were Hilly or Kim. Interestingly, the same dynamics could be found in the Aches. In fact, the Ache women were far more obsessed with food, especially meat, than the men seemed to be. At night I packed away the meat that Kim or Hilly had left over so that I could eat it during the day whenever I was alone. I had to time it just right; if I waited too long maggots would grow all over the meat. I soon discovered that the Ache women and I were not much different after all. They also hid pieces of meat in their baskets and clandestinely consumed it throughout the day.

Several months later I had an interesting experience that made me question, for the second time, the widely accepted egalitarian characterization of hunter-gatherer societies. It was one of my favorite times of the year: "kurilla" fruit were abundant, ripe, and sweet. We spent several days at a beautiful grove, with towering trees, clean forest and a flat, sweeping area.

The first day at the grove I went gathering with several women and picked as much fruit as possible because I was so hungry. When I returned to camp I started to eat as much and as fast as I could in order to go out again and get more for Kim and Hilly. Unfortunately, the feast lasted only a few minutes: an ache woman yelled across camp, with others joining in, that I stop eating the fruit. They said I had to wait for Kim and could only eat more after he had eaten.

While ceasing to eat, I worked to convince myself of the merits of cultural relativism—the belief that the values of all cultures are equally good—to deal with this confrontation, and actually managed to stop eating.

Fortunately, Kim was never as food stressed as I was, so I ended up eating a lot of the fruit after dark. I didn't want to get scolded again.

Besides being concerned with food, I spent a lot of time trying to figure out ways of communicating with the Ache women. I hoped to develop some friendships, but I found that the women weren't very talkative on foraging trips. Walking from one camp to another with huge baskets, children, and pets on their backs, takes a lot out of women. When we would stop to rest, they would lie down or sit alone, sometimes brushing the insects off themselves or their children,eating, or grooming other women. When women forage, they rarely coordinate complementary activities with one another, as opposed to Ache men whose hunting is primarily cooperative. The women seemed to be more social in the evenings, when men and women engaged in lively conversation, told jokes and sang songs. As mentioned earlier, they also enjoyed themselves a great deal when I would unintentionally do very silly things. On my first foraging trip, I sat on the same thorny palm tree trunk twice. The women laughed so hard at this that tears formed in their eyes. Such events made me feel embarrassed and frustrated. But as I learned more about the Ache, I realized that they laugh at each other in the same way.

Peccary, coati and paca hunts were also a great occasion for the women. I only saw women participate in these hunts on four occasions. Women would divide the labor such that one or two would stay behind with the children while the others would help the men locate prey in the thick forest or in burrows.

During these hunts I learned that Ache women know a great deal about hunting, yet they rarely do it.

I saw Ache women come together in yet another and unexpected way. In one of our early trips, when my communication skills were horrendous, I spent the day with one of the more influential Ache women, Vachugi. She had a forceful personality, participated in group discussions and, not surprisingly perhaps, was also physically very strong. We were walking through an area with plants full of small thorns, it was very hot, and there were many mosquitoes. The women stopped to see a dead peccary that the men had just killed. Vachugi sat by the peccary and started singing and crying very loudly. The rest of the women joined in. I couldn't understand what was going on, of course. They held each other and cried while I stood by. Then suddenly, they stopped the weeping completely, as if nothing had happened, and started teasing one another. Later I learned they had been crying over a deceased relative whose name had been Peccary: Chachugi. Interestingly, the same women did not display their grief overtly when a baby died at the settlement: only the mother could do so. Once again, I got scolded this time, not over food, but for crying.

I also tried to learn how to become friends with Ache men. This was trickier because I didn't know what incorrectly timed, subtle behaviors could be unintended sexual invitations. Among the Ache, there are no spatial boundaries between the sexes. There is considerable flirting and touching among men and women who are not married. Men playfully grab women in public, pretending to pull women into the bushes. Women have considerable leverage in these public flirtations, both stopping and initiating them whenever they want. I was never quite sure, however, what behaviors were clearly flirtatious, and what others could be interpreted as serious pursuit. So despite my caution, and very unintentionally, I ended up doing the latter.

After spending several months with the Ache, I started feeling stronger and more comfortable on our foraging trips. I had learned to get firewood with some level of competency, to time data collection, cooking, washing, et cetera in a more manageable way and to communicate better. So I began to take more risks in my interactions with the Ache. I had learned enough key phrases, I thought, to get out of almost any embarrassing situation. On one of these later foraging trips, I decided to try carrying on my shoulders a four-year-old boy whose father had recently been left by his wife. I felt sorry for Javagi because most Ache children are carried by their mothers at that age, and he cried constantly. After carrying Javagi for a while, Bepuragi, a woman of high status married to one of the best hunters, told me to make the child walk, and several other things I didn't understand. I could only tell by the tone of her voice that she was very upset with what I had done. I forgot about the incident until a few days later. After returning to the settlement for our usual period of rest and recovery, the boy's father asked me (in public) to move in with him. He was quite serious, and he also didn't seem to mind that Kim was standing only a few feet away from us. Perhaps carrying a man's son is a form of sexual initiation among the Ache, and Bepuragi had been warning me of this. I don't think I'll ever know.

Two months later we left the Ache. I had a baby, and returned to the Ache for a second visit when she was just a year old. Even though we had nice tents, a generator, reasonable food, et cetera, I was unable to carry out the research project I designed for this subsequent visit. Preoccupied with the cares of motherhood, I had to boil water constantly for her formula, and continually wash and boil bottles and other eating utensils. In spite of this, my daughter Karina had stomach problems constantly. The humidity kept her awake at night, so that I could never sleep more than one hour at a time. During the day, I had to carry her often in order to keep her from wandering off into the forest. She was very attracted to the forest because it was full of sticks that she would pick up and use to dig holes, or hit insects, or anything else that moved. Unfortunately, the Paraguayan forest is full of stinging insects and nettles, and like the Ache mothers, I had to restrict Karina's activities as much as possible. Not surprisingly, I was ill most of the time during this visit. After accomplishing very little, I returned to the United States to write my dissertation.

After I finished my dissertation, Kim and I decided to start working in Venezuela since we could count on relatives to help us with child care and other logistical support.

There, we learned from Roberto Lizarralde, a Venezuelan anthropologist, about a group in southwestern Venezuela that depended primarily on hunting and gathering for its subsistence. Unlike the Ache, the Hiwi are savannah-riverine foragers. They live in the flat, extensive *llanos* of Venezuela and Colombia and take refuge from the merciless sun in settlements protected by the canopies of gallery forests found along the banks of rivers and streams.

The Hiwi economic system appears to fluctuate between brief intensive periods of horticulture and longer periods of foraging. When we first started working with the Hiwi they were full-time hunter-gatherers. However, by 1990, they had planted large manioc and cornfields and consumed few gathered foods.

The first time Kim and I visited the Hiwi we were brought into the settlement by government functionaries working in the local indigenous affairs office. Our journey began in a tractor with several Hiwi who were returning to the settlement after a visit to a small Venezuelan town. The ride took half a day. On the way we befriended a Hiwi man who invited us to stay with his family. We traveled by boat the rest of the afternoon and finally reached our destination: a small village of fifteen families located on a high riverbank, amidst the gallery forest. Our new friend made room in his house for our hammocks and supplies, and within a few minutes we had moved in. We were offered wild roots and turtle soup for dinner, slept well and then spent several days getting to know the Hiwi community.

The Hiwi are strikingly different from the Ache in many ways. There is very little physical contact in the Hiwi society.

Unmarried men and women seem to purposely keep themselves as far apart in space as possible. Girls play only with
girls, and boys with boys. Adult men and women form separate groups such that the women sit together and the men sit
elsewhere. Mixed-sex groups are confined to husband-wife
teams; even adolescents keep themselves segregated along sex
lines. But most interestingly, men and women do not face each
other when they communicate, and rather than speak, they yell
to one another in opposite directions.

I learned about the Hiwi after spending just a few hours
with them. It was already too late: I had broken all the rules
concerning male-female interactions. As an outsider, I got away
with it. Fortunately, neither Hiwi men nor Hiwi women seemed
to be bothered by the way I communicated with the men, so
after two days making friends we tried collecting some census
and demographic data. I conducted interviews using a bilin-
gual informant. We chose a bench under the shade of a mango
tree in the middle of the village. I sat at one end, my informant,
in a very "un-Ache" way, sat at the opposite end. Then the in-
terviewee, an older woman, sat down on a tree stump with her
back to my informant and her face down, about six feet away
from us. When Bawai started asking questions, he would yell
them out and the woman would shout back the answer. Need-
less to say, we deleted all confidential and sensitive questions
from our first "public" interviews. Later we built a small house
where informants could have privacy.

I never found myself in very embarrassing situations due to
the physical separation of the sexes. I spent much of the time
sitting with women, foraging with them, processing food, and
caring for the children. By the time we started working with
the Hiwi, Karina had become a very important member of our
field team. She broke all the rules, and the Hiwi loved it, ex-

cept for one time where she clearly overstepped the boundaries between the sexes. Karina was four years old and insisted she wanted to have a bow and arrow to shoot lizards with the boys. So she asked to borrow these tools and began practicing by shooting arrows at small objects. A few moments later, the de facto chief of the village came to have a talk with me (unlike the Ache, the Hiwi never yelled at me!). He informed me that if Karina played with a bow and arrow, she would be sterile for life. Yesu was very polite, he explained that he did not want to tell us what to do but that the Hiwi did not want to be responsible for this horrible health consequence. Karina was quickly convinced. After having played with many Hiwi infants, she had become very interested with her own reproductive prospects.

I never felt food stress with the Hiwi, and I think that this was partially because the Hiwi are central-place foragers. They have a large settlement where they spend most of their time resting, eating, caring for children and processing raw materials. Most foraging is done within a few miles of the village. This meant we could keep store-bought food in our tents for several months at a time. But perhaps most important, we did not have to accompany the Hiwi on their foraging expeditions to collect data: we needed only to clock them in and out of the camp and weigh all the food. The Hiwi consume very little of the food they acquire in the bush.

Unlike the Ache, the Hiwi have a rich and interesting supernatural world. They felt strongly about protecting us from the evils of the savannah after knowing us for some time. When we first arrived, however, they were not quite sure if we had come from the good or evil side of their supernatural world. One event convinced them of the latter.

In that first boat ride to our friend's village, we opened a small can of sausages and shared them with everyone in the boat. There were several Hiwi from an enemy village who refused to eat the sausages. Later we found that they thought we distributing children's fingers: we were cannibals. Throughout the first long stay in Bawai's village, the children refused to get close to us. We later learned they thought Kim was the devil: Cauri, a tall blond blue-eyed devil. Fortunately, there were enough Hiwi men and women who didn't think we were cannibals, and we can only guess that they convinced other adults. It took much longer to convince the children that Kim was not Cauri.

I think this fear was greatly reduced after my mother, brother and I visited the Hiwi in April of 1986. My mother, Ines, joined me to collect data on parasite load and allergic reactivity as part of a long-term study of Venezuelan populations. We convinced my brother, Pablo, to be our male companion, since it is generally unwise for women to travel alone in remote, rural areas of Venezuela. Pablo, a professional artist, took care of the photography for both projects as well. I was astonished to see how willingly the Hiwi, including the children, cooperated with my mother's request for blood and fecal samples and my brothers' intrusion with his cameras. Everyone was extremely kind to us, but especially toward my mother. It was though, simply by virtue of her age, she elicited a level of respect that Kim and I, and later my brother, never received. The Hiwi danced for her, and the de facto chief gave a speech in Hiwi and Spanish thanking her for her visit. With the Hiwi, at least, it is an asset to take one's older relatives into the field.

Younger relatives were also an asset. In fact, Karina was a star with the Hiwi. At our departure, people showed the greatest concern over Karina leaving. We were told in no uncertain terms that we had to bring her back. Karina's intentions and interests were never questioned, and she was welcome in all the Hiwi households. She had the privilege of doing things with the Hiwi that we could not do because of our age and status in the village. The women loved her fascination with babies. When she was only five years old, the Hiwi women would let her care for the infants. Unlike the Ache, Hiwi girls became skillful caretakers at that age! A real baby was far better than any doll Karina had ever had. Everyone also seemed to tolerate the way she broke most cultural rules: she sometimes sat among groups of men who were snorting the hallucinogenic powder yopo and would ask to stick her finger in it to see what it felt like. Hiwi children usually stayed away from such gatherings. She would touch the sacred Hiwi maraca even though only a few men in the village had the privilege to do so. Karina also spent a lot of time getting her face painted, loved to participate in the Hiwi dances and to bath in the river with the children. Finally, unlike us, she would sometimes join a Hiwi family to go to the bathroom in the savannah. Perhaps because of the evil that lurks in the savannah, no one goes to the bathroom unless accompanied by at least one family member, and usually the entire nuclear family went on these trips. At first, we suspected that the Hiwi had food hidden in the brush that they consumed on these outings, but Karina confirmed for us these were not the picnics we had suspected.

Having a child in the field has been as advantageous as it has been inconvenient at times. And being accompanied on my fieldwork by my child, husband, mother and brother has given me insight into the worldviews of the Ache and Hiwi, and eased my attempts at becoming socially competent enough to communicate with them.

AT THE GATES OF HEAVEN

CHRIS MEARS

WE SHOULD HAVE BEEN WARNED OFF by the cheap cost of the all-inclusive eight-day tour to China. Things started to go wrong right from the start. We were supposed to fly to Beijing via Moscow, but couldn't due to a recent diplomatic confrontation between the British and Russian governments. We were forced to stopover for a day in Islamabad, Pakistan. My hotel lunch guaranteed that I was digestively doomed before arriving in China.

After the 40-hour journey, we were welcomed in China with a meeting and a lecture. Gathered round a large table, sitting on hard, uncomfortable chairs, our group listened to a Chinese gentleman speak very bad English. We were finally served a cup of tea and taken to our hotel.

Our party was seated at a round table with food arranged in the center. One woman volunteered to examine each dish for dog bones. Most of us stuck to eating only rice. This set the pattern for nearly every meal. Fortunately, the rice kept us reasonably full.

One evening, we were taken to the circus and two men in our party were separated from the rest of the group. Unable to make anyone understand they were lost, the pair resorted to mime. This was such a hit with the crowd that they pretended to juggle, tightrope walk and just generally clown around. By the time our guide found them, our men were the center of a large crowd, giggling and cheering them on.

The next day we were off by train on a three-day excursion. The first-class train journey was luxurious, with copious amounts of green tea served. Our destination was an industrial town where the atmosphere was so thick with smoke that the shop doorways had plastic curtains drawn to help keep out the smoke and dust. Hotel windows were permanently sealed with sticky tape. Young women stood by the doors with looks of utter boredom on their faces; it was their job to open doors for visitors. We were proudly shown around a silk factory. The official management lecture assured us that the bored-looking workers were happy to be toiling for the good of the country.

Throughout our stay, we never once saw a wild bird. Here, birds were pets kept in pretty cages by old men who took them for walks on the street. A story circulated that all the wild birds had been exterminated because they were plundering the grain stocks. Our guide vehemently denied this. But he could not explain why we never saw any wild birds.

In the market dogs were kept in small cages, to be bought and made into stew. It was a sad sight. In the medicine shops, reptile and mammal organs were displayed as cures for various ailments, particularly impotency.

In spite of eating nothing but rice and drinking only green tea, I finally ended up in a predicament common to tourists to China, being forced to use a toilet. After joining a long queue, I found myself in a grim, dark and smelly barn with open cubicles and drains separated by low walls. Apparently I was the first Caucasian woman ever seen in such a facility. Of course everyone supplied their own toilet paper.

One day my guide spared me from great personal embarrassment. We were standing in front of a large Buddha statue in the middle of a spectacular palace. The guide told us many people believed rubbing the Buddha's stomach would bring good fortune. Without thinking, I stepped forward and reached up to touch the Buddha's stomach, when one of the armed guards leaped forward. My guide instinctively pulled me away from Buddha's tummy.

Two days before our departure, we found the gates of heaven. A member of my tour group discovered a stand selling cheese sandwiches! Rather stale, on odd-tasting white bread, no butter, with small pieces of sort-of cheddar inside, they were wonderful! That evening, when our guide suggested a collective farm for a "traditional meal" we cried as one, "No! We want to go to the gates of heaven for cheese sandwiches!"

Beefsteak with Onions

Jim Krois

"Wow! This meat is good," I told my wife, Cathie, as I dove into my dinner of beefsteak and onions. "This is the best meal I've eaten in Costa Rica."

Before me sat a thick, tender beefsteak unlike any other I had been served currently, or in three previous visits to my favorite Latin American country. Beefsteak in the tropics is usually thinly cut, and tender because the grass-fed cows raised in the Gulf States are interbred with Brahman Indian cattle. This makes them heat- and tick-resistant, but tough and stringy with a somewhat gamey flavor. Don't get me wrong, Brahman steak, tenderized and fried with onions, is very good, but not nearly as good as what I was eating.

It was the day after New Years 2000 and the world had not ended, at least not in Costa Rica. My wife and I had decided to avoid the hysteria of Y2K by heading to the jungles of the Osa Peninsula in south Pacific Costa Rica. The Peninsula, in an earlier time, had been a place where Panamanians fled to avoid prosecution (or persecution) and live or die depending on their survival skills. The Osa had even turned the Spanish away, making it a sanctuary for local indigenous peoples. In the 1980s, a gold rush remade quiet Osa into Puerto Jimenez, a sordid frontier town of bars and bordellos. When the gold played out in the early 90s, the town turned to ecotourism.

The one paved street in Puerto Jimenez boasted several restaurants catering to Tico and international tourists. Today we were eating at Jossette's, and loving every minute of it.

Cathie enjoyed a wonderful bowl of fresh *sopa de pescado*, fish soup. The waters of Golfo Dulce teemed with fish and local fishermen kept the restaurant refrigerators full, as long as the power worked. The rainy season was over, which meant the power was much more reliable. Life was good.

We chatted about the New Years we had enjoyed at La Capadera, a big ranch on the road to Matapalo. With free beer, soft drinks and a barbeque—who could pass it up?

For the young teenage men of the area, it was a rite-of-passage party as well. This was the time of the year when the young bulls were made into steers. The young men had to wrestle the bulls to the ground, cut out the testicles, then attempt to ride the bull. There were dozens of bulls and dozens of kids. All the proceeds went to the fire pits, where coals waited to cook the fresh mountain oysters.

I watched señoras cut the meat and pop them on the cooking grates. Later, younger muchachos and señoritas passed around the meat wrapped in banana leaves. Everyone was laughing and talking and having a wonderful time.

When the kids came to me with the banana leaves, I politely turned them down. Beer was one thing, barbequed oysters were another. In my world travels I had sampled head cheese, squirrel and camel, as well as miscellaneous mystery dishes. But some things are sacred.

I happily worked on my steak and was nearly finished—two bites left, when I noticed a little flap, more like a hinge, on the end of the meat. Suddenly, I recalled seeing a similar hinge the day before. Somewhere there was a bull that was now a steer, and I had just eaten the best steak in Latin America.

Caught Knapping

Roger Rapoport

FROM THE BANQUET TABLES OF BEIJING to Michelin five-star restaurants in Lyon, haute cuisine always lives on in memory. There are showpiece dishes like Copper River salmon caught that morning in Alaska and served fresh the same night at your anniversary table. And who could ever forget that night in Bologna where the waiter, who knew the kitchen better than you knew your spouse, hid the menu and handpicked the remarkable meal for you.

But to my mind some of the meals that matter most are the ones that can never be repeated because favorite restaurants have closed their doors forever due to exhaustion, retirement or economics. Their names linger in your mind: Warzawa, a steamy red brick palace with astounding Polish food and terrific belly dancers; the Pretzel Bell, the ultimate campus hangout, where the beer always arrived by the pitcher and the hamburgers never let you down; and I'll never forget the ultimate coffee shop, Letz Mangiare, where the penne eggplant was a signature dish.

All personal favorites, all gone. But among these disappearing acts, none can top the loss of Bill Knapp's, a 69-restaurant, 4,200-employee chain that served millions of travelers out of white Cape Cod–style eateries across the Midwest for more than half a century. An heir to the roadhouse tradition, Bill Knapp's was known for its fried chicken and biscuits, meatloaf, bean soup, au gratin potatoes, baked cod, squash and other family fare. It was also a kid-friendly place where,, for 50 cents, you could watch the great gumball machine in the sky unleash golf ball–size spheres that rolled down a 25-foot-long Hot Wheels–style race track into your child's waiting hands.

Giant gumballs were just one of the signature items found at Knapp's. Another was its chocolate cake, always free on your birthday along with a discount corresponding to your age.

One of the great things about Bill Knapp's was that it had the kind of menu and prices perfect for any dinner party. Another plus was customer service. I'll never forget the time the waitstaff managed to miraculously recover my son's lost orthodontic retainers.

Knapp's conveniently located restaurants were a favorite with senior citizen travelers—which persuaded management it had to do something to bring in a younger crowd. The company went for a new slogan, "That Was Then, This is Wow." It added video games in the waiting rooms, introduced cable television, and discontinued signature dishes like apple cranberry salad and chicken croquettes. The striped wallpaper was replaced with bright gold paint and handwritten graffiti-style lettering. The music was cranked up so loud you didn't even need to bring your hearing aid. Without consulting Billy Graham, a beer and wine list was added.

From the customer reaction, you would have thought

Knapp's had suddenly stationed trick-suited hookers in the lobby.

Realizing their mistake, Knapp's began taking out ads to announce the second coming of the chicken croquettes and apple cranberry salad. There were special offers and coupons galore. But it was too late for the 48-year-old chain. The wrinklies who were at the core of Knapp's cash flow were "just saying no" to the chain, with or without its senior discount.

Like monuments on the National Register of Historic Places, you can still find those Knapp's roadhouses remade as realty offices, insurance brokerages and even a restaurant here and there. One such restaurant is the home of an all-you-can-eat sushi bar. At another, in Ann Arbor, Michigan, the building has been painted Darth Vader black, and the burger prices have doubled. Prime Midwestern beef has been replaced by steaks imported from some trendy ranch in California, and they act like they are doing the clientele a favor by selling "artisan" cheeses from unpronounceable towns in Vermont.

All that's left of Knapp's cuisine is the chocolate cake, which is still sold in grocery chains. Sure, there are other restaurants that serve special birthday chocolate cakes. On my wife's latest birthday we found one—an Italian place where the waiters sang a birthday cheer with lots of clapping. But the singing wasn't very good. As my wife blew out the single candle on the wimpy little cake, I thought about where we wouldn't be when my dad turned 101. I wish I could look forward to that day when Bill Knapp's would give him his chocolate cake—and pay him to celebrate his birthday because his 1-percent-a-year discount would finally surpass 100 percent off.

To those readers who may share my nostalgia, I offer the following recipe:

Chocolate Cake in the Bill Knapp's Tradition

1 box (18 oz.) devil's food cake mix
1 1/2 c. warm water
2 eggs

Beat all ingredients together with a mixer on medium-high until smooth.

Pour into a greased and floured 9 x 12 x 2-inch baking pan. Bake 325° for 35 minutes or until tester in center of cake comes out clean. Let cool on wire rack. While the cake is in the oven, prepare the topping.

Topping:
1 stick butter or margarine
1 bag (12 oz.) semi-sweet chocolate chips
1 can (14 oz.) Eagle brand sweetened condensed milk
14 oz. light Karo syrup.

Combine all ingredients in a double boiler over simmering water.

Cook over the simmering water, stirring only occasionally, for about 20 minutes. Remove from hot water and beat with an electric mixer til smooth.

(makes 1 quart of topping)

Cut cake into eight squares and top with a generous spoon of topping while it's still warm.

Top each square with a scoop of vanilla ice cream just before serving.

Store topping in refrigerator, tightly capped, for up to a few months. Freezes well. Reheat in microwave a serving at a time. Bill Knapp's chocolate cake and other recipes can be found at: www.hungrybrowser.com/phaedrus/mostpopular.htm

ABOUT THE AUTHORS

Marius Bosc is a painter who specializes in color and light in San Francisco.

Loretta Graziano Breuning has been a professor of International Business at California State University, Hayward, since 1983 and is a frequent contributor to the *I Should Have Stayed Home* series.

Claudia R. Capos is currently the president of Foreign Accent Inc., an international trade corporation, and the owner of Capos & Associates, LLC., a full-time communications firm, based in Brighton, Michigan.

Mark Cerulli, an award-winning writer/producer at HBO, worked on the promo campaigns of major movies and specials. He has also scripted episodes of two Nickelodeon series—*Hey Dude!* and *Clarissa Explains It All*—produced/ directed DVD "making of" documentaries on *Halloween, Halloween 4* and *Halloween 5*, and co-produced documentaries on the James Bond classics *Goldfinger* and *Thunderball*. When he's not in an edit room, he loves to travel!

Alev Lytle Croutier was born in Turkey. Her books include *Harem: The World Behind the Veil, Taking the Waters,* and *Night Life*. Croutier lives in San Francisco.

Patti Deveney currently works as a career counselor in central Illinois. She is married, with two daughters who have also inherited her love of travel, and remains ever ready for the next adventure!

Bob Drews is a book editor and author of two novels. He and his family live in San Jose, California.

Julia Niebuhr Eulenberg, a native of San Angelo, Texas, had crisscrossed her native state with her parents twice by the time she was three months old. Her passion for travel continues, with a special focus on Europe.

Beth Esfandieri is a self-employed horse trainer living quietly with her animal menagerie on three beautiful acres in Southern California. Although she doesn't get to travel as often as she'd like, she hopes to someday see Scotland, Galapagos, South Africa and Iceland.

Darla Kay Fitzpatrick lives in Four Lakes, Washington.

A. Magdalena Hurtado has been involved, since 1988, in a long-term project designed to study mothering among American ethnic groups. She is currently an Associate Professor of Anthropology at the University of New Mexico.

Larry Jer's ability to say "Why me?" in several languages has been more useful than he likes to admit. Currently following the road well traveled, he and his wife, Jun, enjoy a fixed address in the Pacific Northwest, but will shed their city suits once again when the nomad gene comes out of remission and therapy kicks in.

Andrew Grieser Johns has worked in Amazonia, where this story is located, as well as Southeast Asia and East Africa. He has done extensive research and writing on the conservation of wildlife in logged tropical forests. Johns lives in Cambridge, England.

Joe Kempkes writes film, book and theater reviews online and for an Oakland, California newspaper wherehe lives. Visit his web page at http://www.interlog.com/~kempkes/joe/

Kim Klescewski has edited a number of books for RDR Books, including *I Should Have Just Stayed Home, I Should Have Gone Home, Nine to Five Against* and *Foiled: Hitler's Jewish Olympian.*

Jim Krois is a gray-haired grandpa who grew up in the midst of San Francisco's hippie revolution and, after spending a year and a half traveling around the world in the late 1970s, moved to Oregon. He lives there with his wife, Catherine, and works as a staff photographer for the *Grants Pass Daily Courier.*

Alec Le Sueur completed his four-year degree in Hotel Management at Bournemouth University and left England for Paris to work at the five-star Hotel California, just off the Champs Elysée. Tempted away by the allure of luxury hotels in the Far East, he turned down offers from hotel chains in Hong Kong to accept a post at the Holiday Inn in Lhasa, Tibet, where he spent the next five years. His adventures there are recounted in his book, *The Hotel on the Roof of the World.*

Frank Lev is a longtime San Francisco resident. He has traveled extensively and lived in Japan, Taiwan and Ecuador. He is also a jazz saxophonist and has performed with jazz, salsa, funk, African, rock and blues groups. He currently teaches English to adult immigrants at Serramonte Adult School in Daly City. Other interests include yoga, meditation, body surfing and writing.

Scott Loveridge was a Peace Corps volunteer in Zaire (now Congo) from 1980 to 1982. He is currently a professor at Michigan State University, where he focuses on regional economic development, both in the United States and other countries.

Chris Mears brought up her family on an isolated Rhodesian tobacco farm and then moved to Victoria Falls, where she worked in the tourist industry. After writing about Rhodesian life for newspapers and magazines, she published a book called *Goodbye Rhodesia*. She now lives in Scotland with her husband Martin. They frequently visit their daughters and grandchildren in South Africa.

Marcia Muller is the author of 32 mystery novels, including 24 in the Sharon McCone series. She has also contributed numerous short stories, articles and reviews in national publications. **Bill Pronzini** has published more than 50 novels (alone and in collaboration with others), including 30 in his popular "Nameless Detective" series. He has also edited more than 80 anthologies. He has received two Shamus Awards and the Lifetime Achievement Award from the Private Eye Writers of America.

Karin Palmquist, a freelance writer for newspapers such as *The Washington Times* and *The Washington Post*, loves to roam the globe. She also works as a graphic designer.

Clifford Pierce, a retired PanAm pilot, lives in northern California.

Carole L. Peccorini presently travels and writes with women in Greece and Italy.

Roger Rapoport is author or co-author of 17 books and co-editor of the *I Should Have Stayed Home* series. His books include *Citizen Moore: The Making of an American Iconoclast, Hillsdale: Greek Tragedy in America's Heartland* and *The Getaway Guide to California.* He is currently working on *King of the Road: Trouble Travel Made Easy.*

Edward Reed lives in San Marcos, California.

Janet Roberts was born and raised in Philadelphia, Pennsylvania, and planned to be there the rest of her days. But life had other plans for her in the person of her Marine Corps husband, who came from the water/winter wonderland state of Michigan, where they have made their home since they married 40 years ago. They have two daughters, who both have their parents' weird sense of humor.

Zona Sage has traveled the seven seas and especially loves Paris, Asia and wild jungles. She has published in *Salon, Traveler's Tales* and *Tokyo Family Law Journal.* Sage currently lives in Oakland, California.

Dawn Starin has been studying the endangered western red colobus monkeys in The Gambia for nearly three decades. None of their food items have made it on to her list of "must-have" ingredients.

Hemlata Vasavada emigrated from India in 1968 with her husband and one-year-old daughter. She has a master's in philosophy from the University of Jodhpur. Vasaveda lives in Mount Vernon, Washington, where she is active in Skagit Literacy and Skagit Valley Writers' League. Her articles and humor pieces have been published in the *Seattle Times, Syracuse Herald, Houston Chronicle, Seattle Guru* (now *Planet Guru*) and *Northwest Life & Times.*

Linda Wasylenko was born in Welland, Ontario, Canada and has lived in London, Ontario; Toronto, Ontario; Georgetown, Ontario; Philadelphia, Pennsylvania and currently resides in East Amherst, New York. She is married and has a daughter, a son and three grandchildren. Wayslenko currently works as a receptionist for Region 9 United Auto Workers.